SOFTWARE SECRETS

How To Build Your Own Software Empire
Faster Than You Ever Thought Possible

Garrett Pierson & Scott Brandley

Software Secrets

First published in 2017 by Outstanding Ventures.

ISBN (**978-0-692-96351-7**)

Printed in the United States of America

Table of Contents

Acknowledgements   v

Foreword   ix

Introduction   1

Chapter 1: Why Software?   8

Chapter 2: The Idea   18

Chapter 3: Funding Your Idea   34

Chapter 4: Getting Started   54

Chapter 5: Project Management 101   95

Chapter 6: Beta Testing   119

Chapter 7: Sales Funnels   128

Chapter 8: It's Time to Launch!   136

Chapter 9: Mistakes We Wish We Had Avoided   146

Epilogue   167

Acknowledgements

From left to right: Scott Brandley, Aubrey Barker, Todd Brandley, Garrett Pierson, Cresta Pillsbury, Mike Herz, Duke Brandley, Dave Brandley, Leslie Lovato, Zach West

Although we have known each other and have been business partners for the past ten years, Software Secrets is a unique culmination of our experiences and adventures in ecommerce and software spanning the course of the past twenty years. During that time, a lot of people have played important roles in those adventures, many of whom have spent countless hours working diligently behind the scenes.

This book wouldn't be possible without them.

We would both like to first thank our wives, our parents and our families for their unconditional love and support.

We would also like to specifically thank the following people:

Dave Brandley - Scott's father and co-founder of Trust Guard, Free Privacy Policy, Rhino Support, and Shopper Approved. Dave's support made it possible for us to build Shopper Approved, Rhino Support, and Free Privacy Policy together, and we will always be grateful for that.

Zach West - Lead programmer for Trust Guard and Shopper Approved.

Aubrey Barker - Lead programmer for Rhino Support and Free Privacy Policy.

Duke Brandley - Lead Designer for Trust Guard, Shopper Approved, and Cart Rocket.

Cresta Pillsbury - COO of Shopper Approved Ratings & Reviews, and the best salesperson on planet Earth.

Leslie Lovato - VP of Operations for Shopper Approved.

Paige Larson - VP of Operations for Cart Rocket.

Lindsay Halling - VP of Operations for Software Secrets and Software Funnels.

Todd Brandley - VP of Business Development for Shopper Approved.

Eric Smith (aka 'Johnny Bravo') - VP of Sales for Cart Rocket.

We would also like to sincerely thank the rest of our amazing teams in Ogden, Utah, Orlando, Florida, and Pakistan for all of their hard work and dedication. You are all amazing! Thank you so much for everything you do!

Disclaimer

In order to make Software Secrets read and flow as smoothly as possible, the term 'we' is used throughout the book to describe our (Scott and Garrett's) point of view, or to describe our experiences working on different projects. However, because we love and respect the amazing people we work with, we want to take a moment to clarify that the use of the term 'we' does not mean that it was only the two of us alone that built any of the software companies or products we refer to. We always had a team of incredible people that worked side-by-side with us, who actively contributed to the creation, launch, marketing and sale of every piece of software. We also want to clarify that in a few cases in the book, the term 'we' is used when we were both actively involved in the building and management of a software product, even if we weren't both the owners of that product. Also, in cases where we weren't both involved in a particular company, or there were other partners involved, we've done our best to clarify the context without introducing additional details that would interfere with the storyline.

Foreword
by Russell Brunson

Sometimes I have to pinch myself to remind me that my life is real.

If I hadn't lived it, I don't think that I would have believed it. Just 4 years ago we launched a new software company that went from 0 to over 60,000 active members, with hundreds of new people joining everyday. But, all of this success didn't just happen overnight.

Most people don't know that my software journey started in my college dorm while I was downloading a .zip file.

Back then, .zip files were a big deal, and people we're downloading millions of .zip files of all kinds onto their computers. As I was avoiding doing homework one afternoon, I thought to myself, "What if you could have an advertisement pop up whenever someone downloaded and opened up a .zip file?" That simple little idea led me to create my very first ever piece of software. I called it 'Zip Brander'. At the time I was dead broke, but I knew that I needed to give my idea a shot. I found a programmer in Romania who was willing to try to create the product, and I paid him $20 to do it.

Within a few days it was done, and I gave him an extra $100 bonus because it turned out so cool.

I started selling the product for $67, and sold hundreds of them over the next few months. That idea lead me to my next software idea, and within a year of graduating college, I had made over a million dollars selling these software products and my training programs from my basement.

Fast forward 10 years and my life has been a crazy, non-stop adventure. I've travelled all around the world, I've spoke in front of over 100,000 people, I've met and have become friends with some of the most famous, influential leaders on the planet, I've written several books and have become a #1 bestselling author multiple times, I've purchased my dream home, I've owned a Ferrari (which sounds cooler than it actually was), I've built an 8-figure software company that is improving people's lives and changing the way that products are sold online, and I've helped to both raise and personally donate hundreds of thousands of dollars to help build schools in Kenya, Africa - giving thousands of children an education so they can escape poverty.

Please understand, that I'm not telling you this to brag or boast. If you've ever met me then you know that's not who I am by any stretch of the imagination.

I'm telling you these things to impress upon you the fact that <u>none of this would have ever happened</u> if I hadn't created my first software product, Zip Brander.

Which often makes me wonder...

What would my life would look like today if I had never created that very first piece of software?

What if I never took the risk?

How many thousands of amazing opportunities, experiences, adventures and relationships would I have missed out on over the years?

But even worse, how many lives would have never been changed, impacted or improved in a positive way, if all of the software products I created never existed?

It's a sobering thought.

Fortunately, I don't have to make that decision. But you do.

Right now, you are standing at one of the most important crossroads of your entire life.

You can continue to go down the path that you're currently on, and getting the same results that you've always had.

Or...

You can start your own software company and experience a world with unlimited potential to create anything you can imagine, while becoming financially free, and ultimately giving back and making a difference in the world.

That's why I'm so excited about this book!

'Software Secrets' is like having the master key to unlocking your full potential, and it's packed to the brim with everything you need to know to create your own software empire, faster than you can possibly imagine.

What took Garrett, Scott and I all over a decade to learn in the school of hard knocks, you can now do in a fraction of the time, because all of the strategies, tools, and knowledge you need to succeed are within the pages of this book.

When it comes to building amazing software, Scott and Garrett literally have it down to science. If you want to learn how to build software, I highly encourage you to make them your mentors and follow their invaluable counsel and advice.

They have personally helped me to take my software empire to the next level, and I know that they can do the same for you.

Sincerely,

Russell Brunson

Introduction
by Garrett Pierson

I love Mondays.

It's 6 a.m., and my body naturally wakes up. As I lie there, I try and think of all the things I'm grateful for: my wife, kids, good health, opportunities, friendships, and the list goes on. I wake up with peace of mind, and I'm super excited for the day.

After a few minutes, I roll out of bed and start my morning routine. At 7 a.m. my kids wake up, and I make them some oatmeal. We sit and talk about what they dreamed about last night. I realize that these are precious moments, and I try to savor them.

At 7:30 a.m. I go and put my workout clothes on, and pack my gym bag with some shorts, a t-shirt and flip flops to change into after I'm done.

At 8:30 a.m. I meet Scott (my best friend and business partner) at the gym, and we do our 30-minute, full-body interval training. It's a hard workout, and at the end we're both drenched in sweat, but we both feel amazing. We then grab a protein shake and go on a one-hour walk outside, around a nearby pond, on a path where we have made some of the biggest decisions of our lives. The truth is that over the years, these walks together as both friends and business partners have changed our businesses and our lives in incredible ways.

During our walk we talk about life, family, spirituality, health, and then get into the 10,000 foot view of our businesses and what needs to get done that day. This is where the magic happens.

After our walk we arrive back at the gym, grab a quick shower, and then head to our main office in downtown Ogden, Utah. We usually arrive at the office at around 10:30 a.m. to find a freshly-made, green smoothie sitting on our desks, packed full of fruits and vegetables. It tastes amazing, and gives us the vitamins and nutrients we need to maintain optimal health and efficiency. It's a great way to start the work day.

If all of this sounds a bit idyllic, that's because it is - but it's completely by design. In fact, Scott and I have deliberately engineered our businesses and our lives to work this way – to bend around our will, our dreams and our ideas of how we wanted things to be, and then we made it happen. This 'engineering' has enabled us to create lives where we work on our own terms and time schedules, we enjoy the benefits of financial freedom, and we consistently enjoy a high level of stability in our businesses, our relationships, our family, and our spiritual lives.

Now, before you think that everything in our lives has always been a bed of roses, let me assure that it hasn't. In fact, since launching into the software world, life has definitely had its share of major ups and downs. For example, just three years ago I found myself waking up so sick to my stomach and stressed out of my mind that I wondered if I would even be able to get out of bed. This was because we were about a year into the launch of our new online software business, Cart Rocket, and things were not going as expected. In fact, we were very close to shutting it down and taking a $120,000 loss.

The crazy thing is that during this same time, one of the other software companies we were building, Shopper Approved, was doing millions in revenue, growing at record-breaking rates, and was on it's way to making the Inc. 500 (which happened in 2016). This should have been enough to have me doing backflips, but running a software business, or in our case, running multiple software businesses, is sometimes difficult and often things don't go as we plan or envision them.

Did we end up shutting Cart Rocket down? Did I end up going to the looney bin? No, thank goodness. Instead, Scott and I went on some very long walks, faced some hard realities, picked apart and analyzed everything that wasn't working at the time, and ultimately came up with some very innovative solutions that completely turned the business around.

Even though experiences like these are hard, I know that they're absolutely necessary for growth. Our decisions and experiences give us the ability to learn things that we didn't know even a year ago. And a year ago, we learned things that we didn't know the year before that.

You see, running a software business is one of the most fulfilling things that Scott or I have ever done, and we believe that it's due to all the failures, triumphs and experiences that we've been through. Those ups and downs have molded, and continue to mold us into patient, flexible and understanding entrepreneurs.

At this point you're probably wondering who in the world I am and why you should even care about listening to what myself, Scott or our other business partner, Russell, have to say.

So here's a little background...

Scott Brandley and I (Garrett Pierson) have been business partners for almost ten years. Combined, over the course of our careers, we've been directly involved in the development of over 30 different software products and various ecommerce companies, authored five books, managed multiple offices across the country, employed dozens of amazing people, and have worked with thousands of clients worldwide, ranging from new startups to Fortune 500 companies.

Some of the most popular software solutions we've helped to build are Shopper Approved (ShopperApproved.com), Cart Rocket (CartRocket.com), Trust Guard (TrustGuard.com), Rhino Support (RhinoSupport.com), Free Privacy Policy (FreePrivacyPolicy.com) and Register My Race (RegisterMyRace.com). Together, these companies generate millions of dollars in recurring revenue each year.

In 2016, Shopper Approved ranked #192 on the Inc. 500, making it the 192nd fastest growing privately held company, and the #12 fastest growing software company in America. Then in 2017, Shopper Approved made the Inc. 500 again, ranking #368, which is very difficult to do two years in a row. It also ranked #7 on the Utah 100, which was a great honor. As you can imagine, receiving these awards have been incredibly rewarding and fun. They have also opened up some amazing doors and opportunities.

Russell Brunson needs no introduction, but here's a little bit about the man we call 'The Machine'. Russell is a serial entrepreneur who started his first online company while he was wrestling at Boise State University. Within a year of graduating, he had sold over a million dollars worth of his own products and services from his basement. For over 10 years now, Russell has been starting and scaling companies online. Like us, Russell has also developed several software products and ecommerce companies over the years.

Some of his current projects include the wildly successful software company ClickFunnels (ClickFunnels.com), a supplement company, a coaching company, and he is one of the top super affiliates in the world. Russell is a great long-time friend of ours, and we have partnered with him on various software projects over the years, including Software Secrets (SoftwareSecrets.com) and our newest software companies; Customer Rewards (CustomerRewards.com), and Software Funnels (SoftwareFunnels.com) which you will learn a lot more about in the upcoming chapters of this book.

So why should you listen to us?
The answer is simple.

Together, myself, Scott and Russell have had more successes and failures in the software world than almost anyone else on the planet. These successes and failures have given us something incredibly valuable – **experience**. We know the software world inside and out. We know what works, and what doesn't. We've been down every road you can possibly imagine, including starting businesses, hiring programmers and staff, creating frameworks and infrastructure, overcoming impossible obstacles, resolving billing issues, setting up call centers, sales and marketing, customer support, site design, pricing strategies, SEO, and the list goes on and on... and on.

By combining all of our software experiences together into one book, you end up with an incredible resource that will help you avoid huge problems and pitfalls, recognize and validate winning opportunities, slash unnecessary startup and development costs, and most importantly, dramatically shorten your learning curve. Smart people know that they don't have to experience everything for themselves – they can learn from other people's successes and failures.

Think of Software Secrets as the book that we would write to teach ourselves how to build a successful software company if we had to start all over again. This book is packed full of everything we know you need to succeed in the software world. Does that mean we know everything, and that our way is the only and best way? Definitely not. We are simply sharing with you what has worked for us and what hasn't, and the lessons we've learned from both. It's our step-by-step process of how we create and deliver amazing software to the world.

But there is one thing that we know for sure. Without a doubt, **what you learn in this book will give you the best possible chance of creating a successful software company**. The key is for you to learn and absorb everything you possibly can, and then take action!

This book is different than most books, because it isn't based on any concepts or theories. Everything in Software Secrets is from years of real-world practice and hands-on experience building actual software and software companies from idea, to completion, to millions in recurring revenue, which is why it's so valuable.

Bottom line. If you follow our advice and actually do what we teach, you will be able to create any type of software you can imagine, in record time, and with the best possible chance of success.

Your Software Empire awaits,

Garrett Pierson

P.S. As you continue reading, it will become clear very quickly that we've packed as much valuable, actionable information into this book as humanly possible. But, we can only fit so much into a book format.

For those of you who want a more in-depth experience, we've created a fully-immersive training program that dives deep into the processes and procedures of building a successful software company. In this program, you can watch first-hand as we document every aspect of building our next big software company, Software Funnels, (SoftwareFunnels.com) from start to finish.

We literally recorded everything; the good the bad and the ugly, to give you a real-world experience of what's it's like to build an actual software company from idea to launch. Not only did we video journal and blog the entire process, but we've kept every design iteration, recorded our meetings, made videos of our brainstorming sessions, did weekly podcasts, and took photos of all of our mockups and processes along the way.

The 'Software Secrets Training System' is an incredibly rare opportunity to learn all of the ins and outs of building a real-world enterprise-level software company - directly from Scott, myself, Russell, and our team.

Even if you don't know how to program or write code (we don't either), and regardless of whether you're planning on building an iPhone app or creating the next Google, you owe it to yourself to check out our free introductory video to see how this training can help you become the next software millionaire.

Go to www.SoftwareSecrets.com/training

CHAPTER 1

Why Software?

There are virtually unlimited opportunities in the world today, and each of us travels a different road on our journey to success. With a global economy, the sky's the limit, and if you really wanted to, you could become a real estate tycoon, invest in the stock market, go to school to become a doctor, lock yourself in a room and write your New York Times Bestseller, or do a million other things.

So, why should you go into Software?

Well, the best way to answer that question is to tell you why we chose to go into software.

We both started out selling physical products online in clothing & apparel (Scott) and bluetooth headsets (Garrett). We both did well with these businesses, but they were riddled with problems: fulfilment was insane, shipping costs were high, overhead was expensive, and margins were low. The funny thing is that we both sold off our 'physical product' ecommerce businesses because we knew there had to be a better way to make a living.

We dabbled at being coaches and doing speaking gigs, we wrote some books, we even tried making money with Google AdSense, but none of those things ever seemed to work out or scale. In most cases we found that we were trading large amounts of our precious time for very little money.

That's about the time when we started developing software.

Software is pretty much like selling air. We've often joked about how we have 'unlimited stock' of our software products and how vastly different it is from the old days of selling products, when we had to have inventory and worry about shipping.

That doesn't mean you can't make an amazing living selling physical products, or being a coach or author. What we're saying is that those roads are much harder and take a lot longer than developing software.

Here's why we think software is so amazing:

- You can scale incredibly fast with very minimal resources.
- The barrier to entry is low.
- You never run out of stock, which means infinite inventory.
- There are no physical limitations, which means; no manufacturing, no warehousing, no shipping, and no returns.
- There's no sales tax.
- You make 100% of the revenue on each sale, instead of paying a wholesaler 50-80% and leaving you with the scraps.
- Even if you know absolutely nothing about programming, code, or databases, you can create a software business (we'll show you how).
- Instead of trading time for money, you're able to leverage your time once and make money over and over again, which gives you...
- Recurring billing

- ■ Recurring billing
- ■ Recurring billing
- ■ Did we mention recurring billing? Hopefully, you get the point.

There are a lot more benefits to creating a software product or service, but the number one reason we believe it is so amazing is due to the magic of 'recurring billing'. When you create a service that is so valuable (or 'sticky' in software lingo) to your customers that they are willing to pay you for it every single month, it changes everything.

Let us paint the picture for you...

We'll start out with physical products. Let's take bluetooth headsets as an example.

Let's say that you create an ecommerce website and start selling bluetooth headsets. In order to attract buyers to your site you need traffic, so you decide to pay $1,000 to Facebook and Google to drive traffic to your new website.

As far as the cost of the headsets, you try and save money and hassle, and decide to go with a dropshipper, who takes a 50% cut of all sales, and charges you a $5 shipping and handling fee. (These rates are very conservative, by the way.)

Let's say in the first month you sell 100 bluetooth headsets at an average price of $75, including shipping. That would mean in that month, your total gross sales would be $7,500.

Now, let's look at a software business. Let's say you create a live chat software service, you pay the same $1,000 in advertising costs to drive traffic, and you get 100 customers that sign up and pay you $75/month to use your software. That would mean you made $7,500 in the first month, just like in the bluetooth example above.

You might be saying to yourself, "That looks the same to me, so why is software so great?"

Well, this is where the magic of recurring billing comes into play.

With the bluetooth business, you have two immediate income problems:

First, you have to pay the dropshipper 50% of your sales and the $5 shipping fee. So after the dust settles and you've paid all the costs, including the $1,000 for advertising, you end up with $2,250.

Second (and this problem is way worse), because you have no more income coming in, you have to go get 100 new customers next month in order to keep making the same $2,250 after expenses. It's like being on a hamster wheel and never going anywhere.

However, with the software business, each of those 100 customers you originally signed up not only pays you $75 the first month, but they pay you $75 again the next month, and the month after that, potentially for years to come, which means that you make another $7,500 the second month without having to go and get even one more customer.

It gets even more exciting when we add in the power of compounding. Let's continue the scenario. In the software business, let's say that you continue to get 100 new customers each month. That means that in the second month you would generate $15,000 in gross revenue, the third month you would generate $22,500, the fourth month you would generate $30,000, and in theory, it could continue to keep going up by $7,500 each month indefinitely. (We understand that some customers cancel, which will affect the overall numbers, but we've removed it here to simplify our example. This is called 'churn' and we will discuss it in more detail later on.)

So let's say your software business added 100 new clients each month for 12 months, and each customer paid you an average of $75/month. That means in one year your company would be grossing $90,000/month. Congratulations! You've just created a million-dollar company in one year. Great job!

And where will your bluetooth company be in one year? Still fighting and clawing each month to make $7,500 gross and netting a whopping $2,250 a month, (which by the way, works out to only $27,000 in actual net sales to run the whole company on for the entire year).

But that still doesn't paint a complete picture of the incredible power of recurring billing. For a moment, let's pretend that your bluetooth company gets to keep all their sales and let's look at the total gross sales you've made in year one for both companies:

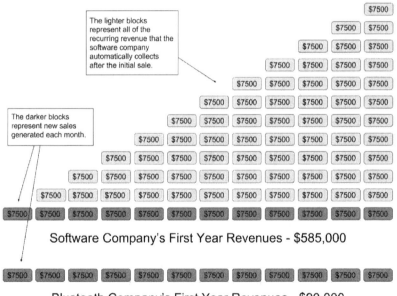

Software Company's First Year Revenues - $585,000

Bluetooth Company's First Year Revenues - $90,000

As you can see, thanks to the power of recurring billing and compounding, your software company made $585,000 in first year, where your bluetooth company did $90,000.

How about year two?

Bluetooth Headset Company - year two: still only $90,000
Live Chat Software Company - year two: a whopping $1,665,000

That means that your software company would make 18.5x more revenue in year two than your bluetooth company would make.

Are you starting to get the picture here?

Are you beginning to understand the incredible power of what what we're trying to teach you?

Recurring revenue never stops! It just keeps building and growing over time.

Bottom line...

Recurring billing is the key to unlocking true unlimited wealth!

And the best part is that it can be done in just a few short years. Take a look at our sales growth chart for Shopper Approved from 2010-2015.

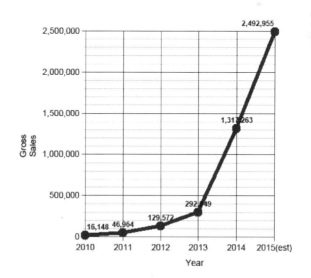

In just five years, starting from scratch, with hardly any money, we built an Inc. 500 company, making multiple millions in recurring revenue. (And we could have done it even faster knowing what we know today.)

As you can see, in 2011, our income tripled over 2010, then it tripled again in 2012, then it doubled in 2013, then it quadrupled in 2014, then it doubled in 2015. Have you ever seen a company that had triple, triple, double, quadruple, double growth year over year? And there's no sign of it stopping. In 2016 it nearly doubled again, and we made the Inc. 500... again!

Well, guess what? Our other software companies are following the same trend. Is it a fluke? Coincidence? Luck? No. It's all directly attributed to the power of recurring billing and a very specific seven-part formula for success that we've created over time as a result of the numerous successes and failures we've had over the years. It's a formula that's worth millions, and we are going to share it with you in the next chapter.

The 4 Different Types of Software

There are many different types of software products or services that you can create, with most software falling into the following four categories:

1. **Web-based software**
    This is software that either runs in a web browser, or supports web browser applications. Examples of web-based software are Facebook, Magento, ClickFunnels, Gmail, Shopper Approved, etc.

2. **Smartphone software**
    This is software that runs on a smartphone via an app. Examples of smartphone software would be MyFitnessPal, Voxer, Snapchat, Angry Birds, etc.

3. **Computer software**

   This is software that runs on your desktop or laptop's operating system. The most common two operating systems are MacOS and Windows. Some examples of computer software are Microsoft Word, iTunes, Avast, Skype, Adobe Acrobat, etc.

4. **Gaming software**

   This is software that runs on gaming consoles like Xbox and Playstation. Examples of gaming software are World of Warcraft, Doom, Mortal Kombat, Super Mario Galaxy, etc.

For the purpose of this book we will be focusing specifically on web-based software that charges recurring billing. This type of software is also known as 'Software as a Service' (SAAS). Please note that even though we're focusing on web-based software, all of the concepts, processes and ideas you learn in this book directly apply to the other types of software as well.

Is Software Right for You?

Hopefully, by this point you're excited to start building your first software solution. But before you become a software mogul, here are some very important questions that you need to seriously ask yourself in order to determine whether developing software is right for you.

First, do you have the desire to build something that can directly impact the market you're going to enter? If you're just going to create something vanilla that 20 people have already created, then don't waste your time. Your software needs to be a game changer in order for it to be successful – something unique, polarizing, or significantly different that stands out.

Second, are you willing to 'Do the Work'? Building software isn't all fun and games – it takes a lot of time and effort, especially up front, in order to get it up and running. Are you ready and willing to follow the steps in this book, and get the right team in place to help you be successful?

Third, are you willing to launch an incomplete product? You don't have to know everything. In fact, you won't know everything, but you have to be willing to deliver a good initial product, fully knowing that it's not perfect, and most likely far from it, going out of the gate. If you can't do that, then you will never deliver and you will waste the next six months or more of your life for nothing. Software is never perfect – it's constantly improved over time.

Fourth, are you willing to have fun and build fun into your product? If you're not having fun, then your product won't be fun, which will show in the quality and delivery of the product. Don't create something just because you need money or because you think it would be cool to have a software business. Create something because you truly want to help your end customer and make the world a better place – just make sure you have a blast doing it!

What about Programming?

A question we always get is, "Do I have to be technical or know how to program to run a software business?"

The answer is a definite "No."

We actually think that it's to your benefit if you don't know how to program. Why? Because this allows you to stay focused on the end goal, and gives you more time to effectively manage the project, helping you to focus more on building the business instead of working in it.

People are often surprised to find out that we have absolutely no programming experience. And while we've picked up some of the basic lingo over the years, we have no desire to program or even learn how to program. What we have been able to do, however, is roll up our sleeves, get down to work, hire good programmers, and get things done.

If you are a programmer, then make sure you read the section 'What if I am a Programmer?' in Chapter 4. There is nothing wrong with you being the main programmer – it may even save you some money. You just need to take some precautions so you that you don't burn out and so that it doesn't affect your ability to effectively manage the project.

If you answered all the questions above positively, then you're ready for the next step - the idea. If you have an idea, then it's time to find out if it has star power or if it's a dud. If you don't have an idea yet, that's okay. Go and grab your thinking cap, and we'll help you discover one in the next chapter.

CHAPTER 2

The Idea

'Great Ideas' can often make you delusional

Just like every other business in the world, our 30+ software products all started out with what we thought was a great idea. And, with each of those great ideas, the more we thought about them, the better they became – until we eventually convinced ourselves that they were the best ideas ever and that everyone in the world would want to buy the products that came from those ideas.

It's great to have enthusiasm and excitement for an idea, but sadly, in most cases, that enthusiasm comes complete with rose-colored glasses. If you're not incredibly careful, those glasses may lead you down a path to frustration and failure.

The purpose of this chapter is to make sure that you are on the right track with your idea. We want you to really think things through and make sure that you have a solid, viable concept before you jump in with both feet and realize that you can't swim.

If you don't have an idea yet, that's okay. There's a section in this chapter that will help you come up with the perfect idea that works for you. And more importantly, once you have an idea, you will know how to determine if it's a winner or not.

The 7 Key Criteria for Software Success

We come up with ideas constantly – it's just that entrepreneurial DNA inside of us. Over the years of successes and failures, as we began to break apart each software product, we started to recognize patterns of certain criteria that our great ideas seemed to have, and that our good ideas lacked one or more of. When we began applying these criteria to our new ideas, the number of these new ideas that contained all the criteria was surprisingly low, but the few remaining ideas that met all the criteria had a much higher probability of being winners.

We want to share with you the '7 Key Criteria for Software Success' that we use to help us to determine whether or not our ideas are worth pursuing. Not only do these criteria help us to quickly sort our great ideas from the good or okay ones, but they also help us to eliminate the red shiny ball syndrome, where every new idea is like a shiny new red bouncy ball that pulls our attention away from what we're currently working on. By having the discipline to table the ideas that don't meet all 7 criteria, we are able to focus a lot more on the ideas that matter and have real potential. This makes us significantly more productive and, ultimately, more successful.

Here are our '7 Key Criteria for Software Success':

1. Is it sexy?

Let's face it – sex sells. But in this case, we're not talking about sexuality. We're talking about the product filling a need or want in a desirable, attractive way. A sexy product has to look attractive, but also bring significant value to the client over time. You have to think of what is in it for them, or put yourself in their shoes and ask yourself if you would really want or need this product, and what you would be willing to pay for it.

For example, if you wanted to build software that targeted online businesses, some of the things that would be sexy to a website owner would be things that make their lives easier, add value, or help them increase their sales. So, with that in mind it would be a good idea to think of creating a software solution that did something like increase their traffic, conversion rate, email opt-ins, return customer rate, overall amount per sale, recurring billing, social media engagement, etc. Software products that meet one or more of these needs are very sexy to that particular market.

2. Is it sticky?

'Stickiness' is a term that is often used in the software world to determine how long a client will use a particular product, (also known as customer retention). The stickier a software product is, the longer the client will continue using it. A good way to determine whether a product is sticky or not is to ask yourself if it would be difficult or painful for a client to stop using it.

Your goal is to try and build stickiness into your software by design, in a positive way that provides ongoing value to your clients. A good example of this is Shopper Approved. Because we collect ratings and reviews for our clients and syndicate those reviews to Google, Yahoo and Bing, the more reviews we help our clients collect, the more difficult it becomes for them to discontinue the service. Our clients inherently understand this, but are fine with it because of the incredible value we provide.

Please be careful how you create stickiness. You don't want to use manipulation or fear tactics to make your product sticky, and you definitely don't want to make it intentionally difficult for a client to stop using your service – that's just being a jerk. You want your clients to *want* to stay because of the incredible value you provide. However, if they do decide to leave for whatever reason, you need to be respectful of their wishes and be a gracious host until the end. One option that we give clients that leave Shopper Approved is to receive a file with all their reviews in it. That allows them to continue to get value from the reviews we've collected for them, even though they're not using our service anymore.

3. Can you charge recurring billing?
We discussed this in detail in Chapter 1, but recurring billing is one of the most important criteria for a successful software product, because without it, you will always be chasing money and be on a perpetual hamster wheel. However, if you are able to charge your clients every single month, quarter or year for your software, you will be well on your way to true wealth.

4. Can you sell it in a call center?
For years and years we relied solely on internet marketing and Pay-Per-Click (PPC) ads to sell our software products with mediocre success, until 2013 when we hired the head sales executive from one of our competitors. With her on board, we took a huge risk and opened our first little call center. It was a total dive and had six seats in a tiny room, but that little office opened up a whole new world of opportunity. Within a year, we expanded twice; we first moved into a second, larger office that fit about 12 agents, and then into a large 3,000 sq. foot professional sales office. We now have two call centers - one in Orlando, and one in Utah - just for our sales teams.

If you wonder how we were able to grow companies to the Inc. 500 level, it's in very large part due to outbound sales from our call centers. It takes some serious guts to do initially, but the payoff can be beyond your wildest dreams. The key is to start small, work out the kinks, prove your sales systems, know your numbers, and then scale slowly. We could write an entire book just on this one strategy alone. Don't be scared if you don't want to open a call center or hire a sales agent – we understand it isn't for everyone - this is just how we do it. There are other effective options that we'll dig deeper into this later in the book.

5. Can you promote it to your existing customers/target market?

This was a hard lesson for us, which cost us a year of our lives and tens of thousands of dollars, so hopefully you can learn from our experience. Once you start to create software for a particular market, if at all possible, keep building software for that market, and specifically for your existing clients in that market. It is 10x easier to sell new, complementary products to existing clients that you already have a relationship of trust with, than to start marketing to a new client base in a market that you don't know or don't have a relationship with.

6. Is it easy to program (6 months or less)?

The key question you need to ask yourself here is, "will it take more than six months to develop my product with one or two programmers?" If the answer is "yes", then it's probably too big of a project, and you should either go back to the drawing board and see what you can eliminate in order to shorten the development time, or cut the idea completely.

Please read the following words very carefully, because we have found them to be true in almost every case. Whatever you think the development timeline and costs are going to be for your project, double them!

Bottom line – a software solution doesn't have to be robust or crammed with bells and whistles to be valuable. Find out what your USP (Unique Selling Proposition) is, and then do what you can to maximize it, especially when you first launch your product. You can always add more features later.

7. Is it customer-service friendly?

This is a lesson we learned from observing a good friend's software company. He had very complicated software that required him to have 15 support staff, comprised of customer support, tech support and programmers. At the time, we were running a similar-sized company with one customer support agent and one part-time tech support agent. Since then, our software business has tripled in size, and we still run it very efficiently with only three customer support agents and two techs.

When considering support and fulfillment, you want to be very aware of what type of resources you're going to need in order to handle your support needs. If you are using Software Funnels to build your software, then we recommend using the 'Help Desk' tool in Software Funnels, otherwise, we recommend using Rhino Support (RhinoSupport.com), which is a live chat/ticketing system we created in order to automate as much customer support as possible. (We'll share how Rhino Support came to exist a little later in this chapter.)

Here is a direct link to a Google Form we made, where you can answer these 7 Key Criteria yourself in the form of a questionnaire - www.SoftwareSecrets.com/7keys

In our Software Secrets Training Program, when we first began teaching our clients about our 7 Key Criteria process, we quickly discovered that a lot of our clients that were just starting out needed different criteria than our clients who had already built successful software companies, so we came up with a beginner version and called it the 7 Beginner Criteria for Software Success.

Here is the modified '**7 <u>Beginner</u> Criteria for Software Success**':

1. Is it sexy?
This is the same as our process.

2. Is it sticky?
This is the same as our process.

3. Can you charge recurring billing? (If 'no', are you sure you can make money another way?)
We always recommend that you charge recurring billing for your software, but sometimes software can add value in other

ways, like creating a 'value add' to an existing complimentary product or service that you already own and sell.

4. **Is there a lucrative, established market that already exists?**
   We discuss this later in the chapter.

5. **Do you see a clear path as to how you could potentially promote and sell this product to that market?**
   You don't have to have your sales process all mapped out this early in the game, but you do need to consider how you are going to get potential customers to find you and buy your product. One of the fastest and easiest ways to do this is to find other competitors in the space who are successful, and then try to reverse engineer their sales and marketing processes.

6. **Will it be easy to program within 6 months or less?**
   This is the same as our process.

7. **Do you have a Unique Selling Proposition (USP) that is so compelling that people will want to buy your solution over other existing solutions?**
   We discuss this in more detail in other parts of the book, but just know that the more unique your idea is, the more you can differentiate yourself from the competition.

   For example, with Shopper Approved, we have three major USP's or differentiators:

   1) We collect up to 70x more ratings and reviews than our competitors.
   2) We syndicate reviews to more places online than any other review company.
   3) Unlike our competitors, we only collect reviews from active, paying customers.

   These USP's have set us apart ever since 2010, and are very compelling reasons for online businesses to choose us over other companies. Now, you don't necessarily need to have 3 USP's, but the more you have the better, and if you only have 1, then it needs to be a real game changer.

These 7 beginner criteria should all be answered with a resounding 'YES'. If there is even one 'no', then you should carefully consider whether or not you should do that idea or project.

Note: If at some point in the future you find yourself in the middle of a project and you happen to come up with a new killer idea that answers 'yes' to all seven criteria, it's going to be very difficult not to get excited and sidetracked. If that happens (and it probably will), we highly recommend that you summon all of your willpower and put the new idea to the side until you have the time, money and resources to take on a new project. You should never start a new project until the current project you're working on is profitable and self-sustaining. That doesn't necessarily mean that you have to have made all of your investment back, but it should be in the process of getting paid back from profits before you start the next one.

How to come up with a Great Idea

For those of you who are reading this book without a great idea yet, the best way for you to come up with your big software breakthrough is to **find a problem.**

Your first step is to realize that there are great software ideas all around you - you just need to recognize them. Typically, you will find that your best ideas come from problems that directly affect your life in some way. To find these problems, put on your detective glasses and start becoming more aware of things that irritate you or annoy you throughout your day, and then think of tools or solutions that would help to resolve those irritations. You can even take an inventory of existing software products or tools that you personally use at home or work, and ask yourself, "What don't I like about this product?", or "How could I make this product better?"

The next best place to look for ideas is within your circle of influence. Look at problems that affect your friends, family or colleagues. One of the best topics of conversation are people's problems - all you have to do is be the detective and probe a little bit. You'll be surprised at what problems you can discover once you start looking for them.

The final place to look for ideas is by being aware of problems that affect the world in general. These are usually discovered by searching forums in markets or industries that you're interested in, reading or watching the news, or even looking at advertisements to see what solutions to problems are being promoted.

If you're really ambitious, you can survey people in the industries or markets that you are potentially interested in by using various online tools like email (if you already have a list), Facebook or Google Surveys, and ask them questions like, "What is the single biggest problem you face on a daily basis?", or "If you could change anything in your industry, what would it be?" Do your best to try and get them to really think about it, and not just give you cookie cutter answers.

Fun tool: We found a cool resource that emails people one new software idea every day: www.nugget.one/daily - this might help you get your creative juices flowing.

Let us share with you an example of how we came up with a software product from a problem we were having. It's actually quite interesting how this idea blossomed into a product.

About six years ago we used the same support staff for both Shopper Approved and Trust Guard, and they were using a help desk solution that only allowed them to manage one company's tickets at a time, so they had to physically close one version of the help desk program and open another version of the exact same program in order to answer the other company's tickets. It was a huge pain and no other help desk system had a solution.

At the same time, Trust Guard was working with a 3rd party company to help manage their security scanning services, and we were having a horrible time communicating. We needed a simple way to track whether specific client's scans were fixed by the 3rd party without having to send a slew of emails back and forth and then track down the answers.

So, after determining that there were no viable options for what we needed, we decided to create a simple email-based ticket system to deal with our own customer support needs. When we say "simple", we mean drop dead simple. It literally took about two days to create it from scratch. The main thing we wanted was a way to log in to one area, and see and manage all our different companies and their email conversations in a support ticket format online.

This is how Rhino Support was born.

It started out as a software product that we needed a solution for in order to solve our own problems. However, as soon as the first version went live, we very quickly realized there were other business owners who needed this product, and so we put some time, resources and money into the software to make it amazing. Now it's a six-figure business that hundreds of companies use for their live chat/support ticket needs. (Here's a dirty little secret. We don't even actively market it. It just grows on it's own and keeps making more and more money.)

You too can look into your business or even your day-to-day life for any problems you might have, and then try to come up with solutions that solve those problems. Once you find a solution to a problem, you'll likely find that a lot of other people have the same problem, and you suddenly have a great idea that you can build into an amazing business.

Validating your idea

The last thing you want to do is spend thousands of dollars and months of your life building a product that no one wants, or creating an amazing product but having a tiny demographic or a cash-poor market. So, you need to spend some quality time up front to really determine if your idea is worth the commitment and investment.

Now, with that being said, by quality time, we mean a week or two, tops. If you have a viable idea, then you should be able to validate it relatively quickly, because in most cases, the information and data you start collecting will naturally support it. If you have a bad idea, then it will be more difficult for you to validate, and will take a lot longer - this is a clear sign that you need to go back to the drawing board.

If your amazing idea has already made it through either the '7 Key Criteria', or the '7 Beginner Criteria', then think of the next 4 steps as the refiners fire. Going through one more round of validation forces you to think deeper about the real impacts and effects that your software will have on both you and your target market.

Believe us when we say that it's way better for you to find the holes in your idea now, then later when you've already jumped head-first down the rabbit hole. This is the moment of truth and you need to be brutally honest with yourself when you answer the questions below.

Now, keep in mind that if you do happen to answer one or more of the questions negatively, that's not necessarily the end of the world. It may just mean that you need to think things through a little more, but it also could mean that it's not a good idea - just be prepared to walk away if you can't truly validate it.

Here are 4 additional steps to further validate your idea:

1. **Determine exactly who your target market is.** This is critical to your success! We discussed this earlier in the chapter, but this is the point where you need to do some serious research and make sure that you know who the customer demographic is that you're going to target, and that it is large enough to support you and any other competitors long-term. If there's any hesitation here, then you need to rethink your strategy.

   When we first launched Cart Rocket, we assumed that our demographic was small to medium ecommerce businesses because that gave us the widest net, but shortly after we launched we quickly realized that smaller websites were much harder to close, weren't willing to pay, had significantly more support issues, and were way more likely to cancel. The problem was that we didn't take the time to really determine who our target market actually was, and that simple oversight almost caused Cart Rocket to go out of business.

   Once we sat down and defined our true target market, which turned out to be medium to large ecommerce companies, we were not only able to 8x our original pricing, but our sales team had way more success, our customer support lowered to a fraction of what it was, and our cancellation rate (churn rate) dropped significantly.

2. **Determine if your target market truly needs or wants your product.** The best way to determine this is to try to find other similar products in your target market and then do as much research as you possibly can about them. If there are multiple companies and they appear to be growing, then that's a

good sign. Try to find any news articles or press releases written about them, and especially if they've received any investments from venture capital firms. You can also search for their domain on Alexa (alexa.com), and see how their popularity is trending. You can even contact them as if you're a potential client and just ask them questions about their company and their growth. In almost every case, they will shower you with a ton of valuable information.

3. **Try to determine if your product is really something that your target market will pay for.** This goes hand in hand with Step 2. In researching competing services, try to determine what the market is willing to pay by what they're charging, and then start from that point. In our experience, when starting out, it's usually a good idea to set your pricing on the slightly lower end of the spectrum, but not so low as to not be taken seriously. Then, as your product improves, your credibility grows, and you start gaining market share, you can raise your prices to meet the demand.

    On the other hand, if you start doing your research and you can't find a solid pricing model to compare to, or if the competitors are giving their services away for free or low cost, or have alternative income models like paid ads or sponsorships, you need to be very careful about entering that market. You can't afford to give away the farm expecting a big payday down the road - it just won't happen. You need to be able to charge for your software upfront, and every month after that if you want to not only survive, but eventually thrive.

4. **Make sure that you truly and genuinely care about your product, and that you're passionate enough about it to seriously dedicate the next few years of your life to it.** Don't just brush this off. This project is going to consume a large portion of your time over the next few years. Plus, in addition to all the

time, talent, money and resources you're going to have to invest, there will be difficult challenges, especially in the beginning, where you won't know how you're going to make it through. You have to truly care about your idea in your heart and soul if you want it to live and breathe, and become a true success.

Malcolm Gladwell said, "When you write a book, you need to have more than an interesting story. You need to have a desire to tell the story. You need to be personally invested in some way. If you're going to live with something for two years, three years, the rest of your life, you need to care about it." The same idea applies to creating software.

Keep in mind that even if you care about your idea, and are excited about moving forward, there may still be doubts and concerns that creep in. Once things get hard, and they will, you will likely start second-guessing yourself, and fear will begin taking hold. As that happens, you will start thinking things along these lines:

"Will this even work?"

"Will people buy it?"

"What if I can't build it?"

"It's going to cost too much."

"There are too many competitors."

"We are too late to the market."

"It's going to take too much time."

Rest assured that these are legitimate questions or concerns that every entrepreneur has considered at some point. For us, this is where going on daily walks helps to keep us grounded in reality. The truth is that sometimes we need to ask ourselves the hard questions in order to ensure that we're on the right path. If we didn't go on walks, our concerns and fears would likely fester and grow like a cancer when things start getting difficult, until it destroyed the project and possibly even our relationship.

In our careers, before we implemented the '7 Key Criteria for Software Success', there were projects that we eventually determined with heavy hearts weren't true winners, and we had to pull the plug on. There have also been projects where we hit huge brick walls that seemed too big to climb over, and we seriously considered quitting, but instead we just kept going on walks and walking and walking... and walking, until we eventually came up with a way to get around the wall, and we ended up taking those projects onward and upward.

With Shopper Approved, for example, there were five big competitors already well established in the market before the first line of code was ever written, and we didn't have any syndication agreements in place with the search engines. That gave us a lot of stress and concern, but it didn't stop us. We knew we had a great idea, and we pushed through our fear and built something better than anyone else in the market. Today, just eight years after launching, not only do we collect more ratings and reviews, and have more syndication channels than any other review company, but we are considered one of the top players in the industry. The reality is that over these past eight years we've had a thousand reasons to quit, but we never did, and if your idea is worth fighting for, you shouldn't quit either.

So, at this point, you're probably thinking to yourself, "There are so many criteria in this chapter that an idea has to pass to be viable, how could any ideas make it through?" That's the point. The reality is that 90% of your ideas won't make it, but that's not necessarily a bad thing. You have to separate the winners from the losers in order to maximize your chances for success.

Don't Get Married until you're sure you've found the Right One

Our last piece of advice to close out this chapter is to remind you that as of right now, your idea is still just an idea. Don't get married to it until it passes all of the validation criteria in this chapter. And even then, it doesn't hurt to get a second or third unbiased opinion. If you have any reservations at this point, remember that there are an infinite amount of other ideas out there – you can still change or even completely scrap your current idea and come up with a better one.

However, once you have committed to a specific idea, and it's passed all the validation criteria, it's time to focus all of your time and attention on that particular one. Marry it! And don't make the mistake of trying to implement more than one idea or project at a time - that's like cheating on your one true love.

Also, remember that you don't have to know everything about your idea right now. That will all come with time. What we have found is that whenever we start a new project, our original ideas are significantly different three months down the road, and by the end of the first year they have evolved into something completely unrecognizable, but much better than what we initially imagined.

For now, having a great, validated idea that you're married and committed to is more than enough to go to the next step.

Note: If you need additional help creating or validating your ideas, we have developed an Idea Generation Workbook with 501 software ideas to help spark your imagination, along with a comprehensive Idea Validation Quiz, that scores every idea out of 100 possible points, so you can more accurately quantify each idea, and compare ideas based on their score. These resources are available in the Software Secrets Training System, which you can learn more about by visiting **www.softwaresecrets.com/training**.

CHAPTER 3

Funding Your Idea

Becoming an Overnight Success

So now you have your amazing idea, it's been fully vetted, and you know you're going to crush it! Before too long, you'll be super rich and you'll be able to buy a private island in Fiji, fly there on your private jet with your family and friends, and live like a king in paradise.

Hey, it could happen.

It's fun to imagine the possibilities, but don't let your excitement cloud your judgement and the reality of the major commitment that you're about to undertake in order to get that island. We briefly touched on this in the previous chapter, but the truth is that making your dream a reality is going to take a considerable amount of time, resources and money.

We're sure you've heard of companies or people that were an 'overnight success'. Well, we guarantee you that if you were to ask that company owner, author, singer or actor, they would tell you a very different story. We did a search in Google for the term 'overnight success quotes', and there are literally hundreds of them. After reading quite a few, a pattern started to emerge, which is that the majority of the 'overnight successes' in the world seem to take about 10-20 years.

Bottom line: there's really no such thing as an overnight success. Yes, someone could become successful in a very short period of time, but generally it took them years to get to the right place and the right time in their business or career for that to happen.

So what does this mean for you and your software business? Should you give up before you even start? No. It just means that you have to be fully dedicated to doing whatever it takes for your idea to succeed. Your time has a price, but software allows you to ultimately leverage your time, which makes it worth the investment. Money, on the other hand, is typically a resource that is limited, especially for a brand new startup, but you will still need quite a bit of it on your journey. Fortunately, there are several different ways to get money.

We have personally bootstrapped all of our businesses, and it has hasn't always been easy, but it was the right move for us. Bootstrapping our businesses has forced us to learn how to run lean, which in turn has helped us to be frugal and maximize our profits over time. Bootstrapping has also allowed us to stay independent, which gives us the ability to completely control our destiny and do things the way we want to do them, without any outside pressure from investors. Over the years, we utilized different types of funding, but we've always paid our creditors back and have tried extremely hard to get all our businesses to be debt-free as quickly as possible.

How you fund your software business is completely up to you, because there really isn't a right or wrong way to do it. Most of the time it comes down to what options are available to you based on your current situation and circumstances. In this chapter we are going to share with you 11 of the most popular funding solutions, along with our input and experiences, and the pros and cons of each one, to help you to more thoroughly evaluate your options.

11 Ways to Fund Your Business

Here are some ways that you can fund your business. They are in the order that we think is best according to our experiences and opinion:

1. **Self-funding** - This is where you initially put in your own money from savings or other investments, and then use the business profits to fund the growth. According to Entrepreneur.com, 80% of startups were self-funded in 2014. This is our #1 choice if you have savings that you can afford to invest.
   - Pros - You don't have to account to anyone, which gives you ultimate flexibility and control over your future.
   - Cons - It can be a struggle to get up and running. You have to be frugal and run super lean so you don't run out of funds.

2. **Negotiate an advance from a strategic partner or customers** - Scott's brother used this option to start his software company. He saw a need for software that tracked solar panel sales from the initial sale through to the installation, so he approached a local solar company and sold them on the idea. They ended up funding most of the project so they could use the software once it was completed.

   Another of our clients is in the chiropractic business. His plan is to reach out to his network of chiropractors and offer them lifetime access to his new software in exchange for an upfront investment. They end up saving thousands over time, and he gets the funds he needs to fully develop the software.
   - Pros - You can leverage the money of someone else who has a mutual interest in your software.

■ Cons - You might lose some control over the project, because you are forced to build the software to the funding company's needs and specifications. If you go this route, try to avoid giving up ownership if you can. Try instead to give them lifetime access, or create a way to pay them back over time. Be creative.

3. **Join a startup incubator, accelerator or contest** (for example, Y Combinator, AngelPad.org or Launch.co) - These are companies that invest in new startups and help you optimize your product before launching. However, in order to go this route you need to be up and running to some degree.

   ■ Pros - You get a team of experts on your side, helping you to optimize your software, design, processes, delivery, etc. They can help you avoid a lot of pitfalls and introduce you to bigger investors to help take your business to the next level.

   ■ Cons - You give up a piece of your company (i.e. freedom and control), and you typically have to move to their location for a few months to be mentored and trained. After they've taken their piece, they introduce you to another round of funding. Those investors take an even bigger piece, which increases the pressure to deliver, while further lowering your ownership, freedom and control.

4. **Apply for a small business grant** (for example, Grants.gov) - The grant process is long, but may be worth pursuing if you're going into the right business or live in the right location.

   ■ Pros - If you manage to get a grant, you get to keep all the money without having to pay it back or giving up any equity.

   ■ Cons - Grants tend to take a long time to get, and have very specific requirements that you have to follow both before and after you get awarded.

We actually have a Shopper Approved competitor in the customer rating and review space, who was able to get a $600,000 grant from the National Science Foundation to build their company. Who knew you could get a grant for collecting ratings and reviews? If we would have know that was available to us when we started out, that would have been a huge game changer! So, the moral of the story is that it doesn't hurt to do a little bit of research and see if there are any grants out there that could help you get started. (If you're going to look into this option, your best bet is to hire a freelance grant writer on upwork.com to help you research and write your grant applications.)

5. **Start a crowdfunding campaign online** (some examples are Indiegogo, Kickstarter, and GoFundMe) - Traditionally, this has been a very popular way to fund and launch new product-based companies. Software companies, on the other hand, have proven to be a bit more challenging, but that doesn't mean that you can't make it work. Many software companies have raised money through crowdfunding.

- Pros - You get to keep the money if the project hits or exceeds the funding goal (after crowdfunding fees), and you don't have to give away any ownership in your business. You also get a list of customers to start with, that can test your software and give you feedback, reviews, and ultimately, testimonials for your launch.
- Cons - You have to pay a portion of the pledged money to the crowdfunding service, and you have to give those new customers who pledged money something of value in return.

If you're going to attempt this option, you should know that the software campaigns that tend to get the most traction are consumer-focused productivity apps or games (where consumers are the end users), as compared to business-focused solutions (where business owners are the end users). But, that being said, it never hurts to try, especially if you already have an existing customer base or following that you have influence with.

6. **Get a loan from friends or family** - These are typically the easiest loans to get, because you can leverage an existing relationship. If you choose this path, make sure you put together a nice presentation, and know in advance what amount you're going to ask for, along with the payback terms. Make sure to put an actual loan agreement in place, and do your best not to give them ownership if at all possible.

   ■ Pros - There is typically a very fast turnaround to get the money, sometimes within a day, and you don't have to qualify or fill out application forms.

   ■ Cons - If you don't pay the money back, you can destroy relationships. Our advice and personal philosophy is that if for some reason the venture fails, you should still try and do everything you possibly can to pay back your obligation, even if it takes several years. Your integrity is more important than any amount of money, so if you make the commitment, keep it.

7. **Use credit cards** - This is something we've done many times in the past, but it comes with a price.

   ■ Pros - You get flexibility and keep full control of the company. You can also make larger purchases and minimum payments over time.

   ■ Cons - It can put a lot of stress on both your business relationships and personal relationships if the money isn't paid back or if the company struggles to make a profit.

8. **Get a bank loan or small business loan** - This can be a difficult road to travel initially, due to the fact that most banks won't lend you any money until you're making some. If you go this route, try and get a line of credit instead of a loan. That way you only have to make payments on what you actually borrow. (Once Shopper Approved was making money, we were able to secure a $100,000 line of credit that allowed us to open our first call center.)

- Pros - You keep your ownership intact and can typically get access to larger amounts of money.
- Cons - There are usually a lot of hoops to jump through in order to get approved, and you have to pay it back with interest.

9. **Trade equity or ownership for startup help** (for example, giving someone sweat equity in your company in exchange for their time or expertise) - We've been down this road more than once, and it's never worked out. Our advice is to pay everyone a wage if at all humanly possible and never give out equity, because the reality is that in most cases, the people you bring on need the money and won't be able to afford working for you for free for long, which means that they will eventually start coming up with excuses, slacking off and avoiding you. Once this happens, relationships become strained, making things very awkward, and ultimately stopping your project in its tracks.

   If you're going to give anyone equity, including your best friend or someone who wants to be a part of your project, don't do it under any circumstances until they've met very specific, measurable milestones, and have proven to you without question that they are in it to win it for the long haul. If you give out any equity prematurely, we guarantee that you'll regret it down the road.
   - Pros - You *might* get some initial work done towards building your software.
   - Cons - You'll *very likely* get screwed over, become super stressed out and frustrated, and give up ownership for nothing.

10. **Angel investors** (you can check out Gust.com to find a good fit for you) - The good thing about angel investors is that they don't

necessarily want to be involved in your project, but unless you have a pedigree from Harvard or Stanford, they probably won't give you the time of day until you're making serious money. Angels are more of a longer-term play.

- Pros - They can give you big money to go to the next level, and don't really want to be directly involved in how you run things.
- Cons - You will have to give up equity, and you've got to already be successful before an angel will take you seriously.

11. **Venture Capital investors** (Fundingpost.com and Nvca.org are good places to start) - Venture Capital (also known as V.C.) is very similar to angel investing in the sense that they won't give you the time of day unless you're already successful. We don't recommend this route, mainly because you ultimately give up control of your business in order to go to the next level. They won't come out and tell you that directly, but when a V.C.'s millions are on the line, you can rest assured that they are going to be watching you like a hawk. You will have to account for everything you do and every penny you spend. In our opinion, freedom is more valuable than money.

- Pros - Big money and connections can dramatically accelerate your growth in ways you can't imagine.
- Cons - They take a big piece of your company and a lot of control. You ultimately give up your freedom in exchange for growth opportunities.

Again, these are in order of how we suggest you try to fund your idea. Who knows? Maybe your business is already up and running, and you should go for venture capital. Or maybe you're broke and your only option is to get a loan from your rich uncle. We simply want to give you a solid starting point on what we feel is the safest route to success.

Bootstrap Funding Vs. Investment Funding

Since we're on the topic of venture capital, for some reason, most people think that once they come up with an idea, an investor is going to jump on board, give them millions to help their business grow, and they will be rich. Well, the sad reality is that only a tiny fraction of companies ever get V.C.. Some do, but when they eventually sell, the owner doesn't get much more than what they would have got if they had kept their company small. This is mainly because of the enormous amount of equity they had to sacrifice to get to that point. So, just for fun, we thought we would throw in a comparison between bootstrapping and getting an investor.

Pros of bootstrapping:

- You own 100% of the business.
- You keep 100% of the profits.
- You get to make the decisions.
- You can innovate faster with less red tape.
- There's no stress of trying to make investors happy.
- There's more room for creativity.
- It's more efficient, since you figure out how to do more with less.
- You can do anything you want - you're the visionary.
- The only timelines that must be hit are set by you.

Cons of bootstrapping:

- There is a lot of personal risk because you're responsible for all the financial decisions.
- You could end up with a significant amount of debt.
- The growth is slower because you have to reinvest your profits in order to grow.

Pros of investors:

- You get a large influx of capital.
- You have access to industry leaders and high-level mentors that you wouldn't otherwise have access to.
- You have the ability to hire more resources faster.
- The growth can be exponential.

Cons of investors:

- Investors set the bar very high.
- You have to give up a lot of equity and control.
- There are many strings attached.
- There's a lot of red tape and bureaucracy.
- Your business is instantly and always for sale.
- Investors primary concern is their Return On Investment (ROI) not the customer's needs.
- Your decisions are monitored and limited.
- You have to account for everything.
- Stress increases from trying to make investors happy.

How We Did It - Cart Rocket

As we said before, we've chosen the bootstrap method of funding for all our businesses. We can honestly say this was the best way for us because it fit our personalities and the direction in which we wanted our businesses to grow.

The reason we believe that bootstrapping is the best option is that when you are first starting any new business, no matter how prepared you are, you really have no idea how things are going to go; you don't understand what your market really wants or needs, you don't know how a market is going to react, you don't know how to price your services, and a hundred other unknowns.

We find that bootstrapping forces you to run lean and make more conservative moves initially, to make absolutely sure that you're building something that people really want or need. In most cases, it's much better to go slower at first, and make smaller, more deliberate moves, because you avoid problems down the road.

A great example of this was Cart Rocket. We launched the first version of our website and cart abandonment software company in 2014, and we did the best we could with the information and resources we had. It wasn't until nearly 14 months later that we felt like we had our pricing and services dialed in correctly for our market. Over that time, we significantly raised our prices, and made several significant improvements to our product that more than justified the price increases.

Even in that first 14 months, we took some risks and made some bad decisions that cost us a lot of money and almost shut down the company, but if we had got a big investor upfront, they would have expected us to move much faster than we did. Looking back, that would have been a complete disaster. Starting a successful software company takes research, time, hard knocks, trial and error, and falling down and skinning your knees and elbows a few times before getting a true grasp of the direction your business needs to go in.

Some of you might be asking yourselves, "What if I go down the bootstrapping path and run out of personal savings?" Well, the reality is that for most people that's probably going to happen. During the development of Cart Rocket, we ran out of personal funds for a time, and were forced to go down the funding list mentioned earlier in the chapter in order to find additional sources of money. Ultimately, by the time we ended up getting Cart Rocket back on track and profitable, we had ended up using our personal credit cards, business credit cards, family loans, and even revenue from our other successful software companies. Sometimes when you have a dream and a worthy goal you have to get creative to keep it alive.

How Much Will It Cost?

We wish we could say, "You only need X amount of money to complete your project and that should do it." The reality is that we can't actually give you a number, because every software project is completely different, and it totally depends on the scope of your idea, how fast you can get it to market, how well you manage your resources, and several other factors that we will help you navigate throughout this book.

For example, you can literally build a piece of software for as little as $200. It will probably only solve one problem and it will be difficult to charge recurring billing for, but that doesn't mean people won't buy it.

Our partner, Russell Brunson, actually started his career by building out simple software tools just like this. They would typically cost him less than $200 to build, and then he would sell them to customers for anywhere from $50 to $200 each - talk about a return on your investment! In fact, his very first piece of software only cost him $120 to create. He went on to built several other inexpensive software tools, and made millions from them.

On the other hand, if your project is larger in scope, then you could easily spend tens of thousands to build out a robust software solution. We tend to build software on this level, where we're creating solutions to bigger problems. Every time we build a software company, our goal is to launch it and then get it to the point where it can completely run by itself and pay for itself without us being directly involved. This means it needs to be able to pay for a project manager, full-time sales and support staff and other part-time staff or independent contractors, like designers and developers. As you can imagine, once a company reaches this point, things get really exciting! This is where the dream of time and financial freedom start to become a reality.

So, whether you build apps or tools for a few hundred dollars, or larger software solutions for thousands, there's one key strategy we've learned that will help you save a lot of money while allowing you to launch your software as quickly as possible.

The key to sticking to a budget and saving money is to create the first version of your software with the minimum amount of preferences, functionality and features. This is called your Minimum Viable Product (MVP). To build an MVP, you first build out your basic core feature set, and then add additional features and options *after* you launch. This is extremely hard to do, but it is an absolute must if you want to get started as quickly as possible without breaking the bank.

In order to minimize your costs, it is important to get to market as soon as you possibly can. Launching something minimalistic that's good quality and fast to develop, is 100 times better than launching something that is feature-rich, fully polished and slow to develop. The feature-rich, fully polished version can still happen, but you can do that after you've launched version 1.0 and are making money.

To help you come up with some estimated cost and timeframe figures, we created a software development estimation calculator, where you can enter in a few data points and it will give you some estimations as far as overall cost and development time. To access the estimation calculator, go to www.SoftwareSecrets.com/estimate.

Trading Equity or Ownership for Startup Help

One of the funding options we mentioned earlier was to trade equity or ownership for startup help. We highly suggest you shy away from this. We've tried this over the years in different forms and situations, and in every single case it has caused us a lot more problems and stress than we ever imagined.

There are a lot of reasons why this is a bad idea (which is why we wanted to expound on it a bit more), but here are the main ones.

- **People are really bad at setting expectations.** When you first share your idea, it is easy for both you and whomever you're sharing it with to get excited and caught up in the moment. But unfortunately, once bills start piling up for both the business and at home, excitement wanes and people start to magically vanish! The reason this happens is that when there's no money coming in, then there's no immediate return for the amount of time they are spending on the project. People get discouraged and quickly realize just how hard it is to start a business. This path ultimately leads to an extremely long and potentially indefinite production time, major stress, hurt feelings and damaged relationships.

- **People feel entitled.** Before we were partners, Scott and his dad had a programmer who had been with their company from the beginning. He was such a hard worker and so loyal, that they gave him 5% of their company as a gift. Over time, as the company made more and more money, that 5% turned from an act of kindness into a curse, because every time they made a purchase or spent money to help grow the company, the programmer questioned them. After all, any money being spent meant less profits, and a smaller distribution to him. It was a classic example of the tail wagging the dog – all over 5% that they gave him as a gesture of kindness.

Ultimately, they decided to buy him out and paid him tens of thousands of dollars. It was money they really didn't have at the time, but they had no choice – they had to get their freedom back so they could build the company without their decisions and motives being questioned. (Just as a side note, they don't have any hard feelings toward this programmer – it wasn't his fault. It was just a natural reaction to the situation. The reality is that no one thinks of that type of scenario going in, so hopefully you can learn from their mistake.)

- **People are busy.** We have another really good friend, who is a genius at marketing. We had just launched one of our software companies when he found out about it and was so excited that we ultimately became partners. We agreed to continue to build and support the software, and he agreed to head up the sales and marketing. The only problem was that our friend already owned a successful software company of his own, and was very busy building that company. As you can imagine, days turned into weeks, and weeks turned into months, with very little progress made in the marketing department. Ultimately, we decided that in order for the company to move forward, we needed to part ways, so we pulled all the profits made to that point and bought him out. It was hard and painful to go through, but it was the right decision. Fortunately, we were able to remain great friends, but that doesn't always happen.

Ultimately, we've found that if you have the funds to pay for people to help you, then you should. You'll find that you get a lot more done in a much shorter time period, and you keep your freedom intact. When you pay your help, your project will go a lot more smoothly, and you will always be in control.

If you do end up deciding to give up some equity or ownership, then we highly recommend you really sit back and think of all the potential consequences. Be very methodical in setting the expectations and create written agreements/contracts that lay out exactly what is expected of each person, with very clear milestones that must be met for their ownership to vet. Get legal help from a lawyer if possible. You will regret it down the road if you do not set the bar high and get something in writing!

What About Partners?

Another important point to consider is that you may have the opportunity to partner with someone; more than likely a friend or family member. All we can say about this is to be extremely careful. Just like in the previous section, where we went through the potential pitfalls of giving someone equity in your business, we want to warn you about the potential pitfalls of a partnership.

Why pitfalls? Because many partnerships end up in disaster.

Here are what we believe to be the top five reasons partnerships fail:

1. Bad communication
2. Unhealthy communication
3. Infrequent communication
4. Defensive communication
5. No communication

This list might sound ridiculous but we want to really stress the point what we strongly believe that without proper communication, failure is almost guaranteed.

Just like a marriage, a business partnership is all about communicating needs, desires, feelings, frustrations and more.

We have been business partners for ten years now, and there have been occasions when we've had our differences or even got into arguments. However, overall we have a great partnership, which is due to the fact that we are both good guys trying to do the right things, and we actively communicate every single day.

As we mentioned in the Introduction, we go on a walk each morning where we talk about life and business. This is where our communication is at its highest level and where we are able to communicate our frustrations, fears, goals and feelings... in a manly way of course.

Another thing that helps us is setting expectations. What we mean by this is that we know exactly what we expect of each other, and we trust that each of us will do what we say we will do. Trust and setting expectations are the bread to the butter of communication.

So let's say you decide to bring in a partner. What percentage of the company will they get? We (Scott and Garrett), own each of our businesses 50/50. The reason that we split everything 50/50 is that we know and trust that we will both give an equal, fair share of our time and effort to each business.

This, however, may not be the case with you and your business, so you need to figure out what works best in your situation. A lot of times, the answer as to what you should do can be unclear, so try to focus on how you feel, and then try to do what your gut tells you to do – it's usually right. Don't just make bad decisions in order to not hurt someone's feelings. It's better to rip off the bandaid now and have a little pain and discomfort, than to wait and try to plug a gaping wound later.

Here's what James Altucher, author of the book 'Choose Yourself', has to say about how to determine how much equity to give a partner or partners: "Divide things up into these categories: manage the company; raise the money; had the idea; brings in the revenues; built the product (or performs the services)." He then says to divide the equity up into equal portions depending on the answers to those categories.

Also, here is a handy calculator we found that may help to know how much equity to give, if you have a group of people who all want equity in the business: Foundrs.com

Once you have decided, all parties must agree and be 100% content with the arrangement. As we stated before, this should be written in a legal document with all the percentages and expectations clearly designated, otherwise it will come back to bite you down the road. (Once again, add milestones and contingencies in case things don't work out, especially if you're bringing on a partner. There's nothing wrong with having their percentage vet once they've put in the time or have proven their worth.)

Setting up your Accounting and Business Structure

Once you are ready to move forward either on your own or with a partner, it is time to set up the business.

If you are on your own, we suggest that you just set up your business as a sole proprietorship to keep things simple and easy initially. You alone own the company and are responsible for its assets and liabilities. There is nothing really to set up legally other than a business license, but we highly recommend setting up a separate bank account and having all funds related to the business run through that account. It's never a good idea to mingle business and personal funds. Also, remember to set aside taxes when you start paying yourself a profit. We recommend setting aside 25% of all net income, which is the income left over after all expenses are paid but before you pay yourself. You can also set up a DBA name (Doing Business As) so that your business can have a name other than yours. We are not experts in this area, so we suggest you seek out a lawyer and/or CPA to set this up correctly.

If you have one or more partners, then we highly suggest that you set up an actual business entity. To do this correctly, we recommend that you consult with a lawyer. If you set things up properly at the beginning, then it will make things way easier down the road when you start making the big bucks.

A big mistake we made when starting out was not keeping track of our finances properly. Because we never knew the real numbers, we estimated and guessed a lot of the time, which got us into a lot of financial trouble. Ultimately, we got to the point where we realized that we had dug ourselves into a big hole. Fortunately, we smartened up and hired a part-time bookkeeper, which had an immediate positive impact on our business. Since then, we've met with our bookkeeper religiously once a month, and we go over every transaction and report, so we know exactly where our money is and where it's going. Fortunately, bookkeepers are relatively inexpensive, which means that you should get one as soon as you start making money. Bookkeepers not only take care of your finances, but they can also handle your payroll and prepare all your financials to give to your accountant at the end of each year.

We use Majesticpayroll.com for all our bookkeeping and payroll needs, and we use Eidebailly.com as our CPA firm. Both companies have been amazing to work with, and we highly recommend them, however, it should be relatively easy for you to find a local bookkeeping and CPA firm in your area.

Another question you might be asking yourself is whether or not you should pay your staff as W2 employees or as independent contractors. We've had a lot of experience in this area, so we'll try to make it easy. If your staff member is outside of the USA, then generally they can be an independent contractor, which means they are in charge of paying their own taxes. If the staff member is in the USA and is a key part of your business, then we highly suggest you pay them as a W2 employee - especially if they work in your office. If they don't work in the office and have a legitimate business where they work for other people besides you, then you can justify paying them as an independent contractor, but that's rare. When we first started hiring people, we paid a lot of our staff members as independent contractors, but over time it became too fine of a line with the IRS. Ultimately we decided that we would pay all U.S. staff members as W2 employees. It costs about 15% more to do it that way, but it helps your staff keep track of their taxes and it lets you sleep at night. Also, don't try and pay your staff yourself.

Always use a payroll company. They are super cheap and incredibly good at what they do. We use ADP for our payroll and highly recommend them.

Don't let this stuff take a lot of your time. Get it set up all upfront and then get to work building your software. The key is to get help with things that you're not good at or that you can outsource to people who know what they are doing. Outsourcing your business setup, legal documentation, bookkeeping and payroll are totally worth the money and make your life a million times easier.

Note: in our Software Secrets Training System we dive deeper into how to properly set up a business, and we also interview Josh Bauerle, the founder of CPA on Fire (CPAonFire.com) where he shares several accounting and bookkeeping strategies. To learn more about the Software Secrets Training System, go to **www.softwaresecrets.com/training**.

CHAPTER 4

Getting Started

The 12 Steps to Building Successful Software

In this chapter we dive into the actual conception, planning and preparation stages of your new software product. When you're just getting started, it is very important that you get things right, and that you do things in the right order.

Over the years, we have done almost everything wrong that you can possibly imagine when it comes to software, but fortunately, we very rarely make the same mistakes twice. Ultimately, through it all, we have come up with 12 Steps that will help you to get your project up and running as quickly as possible.

These 12 steps are everything you need to do <u>before</u> you start programming your software. If you follow these 12 steps, you will be able to fully understand the entire scope of your project, dramatically slash your timeline, and significantly reduce your development costs.

Here are the 12 Steps to Building Successful Software:

1. Brainstorm 'why' your idea should exist
2. Buy a domain name

3. Design your logo

4. Set up your Software Funnels account

5. Brainstorm and Mind Mapping

6. Wireframe Mockups for your designer

7. Hire a graphic designer

8. Design pages

9. Hire programmers

10. HTML/CSS development

11. Set up Hosting & Servers

12. Create an opt-in page

In this chapter we'll cover all 12 steps, which makes it a bit on the long side, but it's packed with really valuable information, so we hope that you'll forgive us for it's length.

Before we get started, we want to share with you a secret that will have a huge impact on your overall success.

The Secret to building great Software

Would you like to know one of our best kept secrets to building amazing software? Here it is:

Design first and program last.

This may sound obvious at first. In fact, you're probably thinking to yourself, "That seems like common sense. Why would you do it any other way?" Believe it or not, when it comes to building software, most beginners throw common sense right out the window, and do the complete opposite of what seems logical.

What we've found over the years is that people who try to build software get so excited about their idea, that one of the first things they do is hire a programmer. They don't have a plan, they don't have a development strategy, and they don't even know how the software will work, what it will look like, or how it will flow.

In our experience, one of the keys to our success (and yours), is to build the proper foundation for your software by first wireframing, then designing, and finally programming. You first need to wireframe the entire flow of your site, mocking up a rough draft of every single page that a user will utilize, from the signup process to the backend/control panel. Then, once you have these wireframe mockups done, you need to send them to a designer to design each page as if the software already existed. Once the entire backend is designed and done, only then do you get programmers involved.

This one secret has saved us countless hours in the development process and it will for you as well. The reason you need to do it this way is that it literally cuts in half the amount of programming time that you would normally have to allocate, because by giving the programmer the exact layout up front, they don't have to try to guess what your vision is, because they can see it in real life.

Think of it like this...

Programming the traditional way is like giving someone a piece of blank paper and asking them to draw a mythical creature that you have pictured in your mind. They've never seen it before, but you are going to try and describe it to them, and have them draw it. As you can imagine, what you envision and what they create will likely be very different, and take many iterations before it begins to even look remotely like your vision. Compare that to giving the same person a piece of paper with a 'color by numbers' picture already on it. The image of your creature has already been drawn to your exact specifications; they just have to color the numbers to make your creation complete.

The reason we wanted to share this secret with you now is because it will help you to understand the order and reasoning behind the

12 steps. Each step is in a very specific order, to help you get up and running as quickly as possible.

Note: In our Software Secrets Training System, we have a checklist to help you keep track of where you are in the process, and we discuss the 12 steps in more detail.

Go to www.SoftwareSecrets.com/training to learn more.

Step 1 - Creating Your 'Why' Statement

Creating your 'why' statement is critical because it allows you to create the foundation on which you'll build your company culture around. It will be the driving motivator behind your actions, both now and in the future. It will also help you to solidify your software's purpose and place in the world.

To complete this first step, we recommend that you set aside at least an hour of uninterrupted time in front of a whiteboard, piece of paper, or your computer.

During that time you need to ask yourself this question:

Why should this software exist?
Sit down and write down every reason you can possibly think of as to why your software should exist. Once that's done, ask yourself the following additional questions and write down everything, whether it's silly, outlandish or redundant. This step is very important. Even if you think you already know the answers, just do it anyway.

Who is it for?
Why will it be better or different than the competition?
What will be your Unique Selling Proposition (USP)?
What problems does it solve?
Why do you want to build it?
What is its purpose?
How will it affect the lives of the people who use it for the better?

Once this step is complete, you need to spend some quality time figuring out how to take everything that you just wrote down and put it all together into a one-sentence statement. This sentence should explain why your software should exist.

This is going to be extremely hard, but it will be worth it. You must know why the product or service should exist in order to start the process. Think of it as your mission statement. This will be the reason why you're going to get up in the morning and stay up late for the next few months, or even years. This is the reason why you're going to invest your hard-earned, valuable time and money to make something amazing.

Here are some warnings:

- Don't spend more than an hour.
- Don't exceed the one-sentence limit.
- Don't worry about it being perfect (you can always adjust it later).
- Don't start thinking too far into the future of how you will market or sell the product/service.
- Don't skip this step.

Start your sentence with something along these lines:

"This business will exist in order to..."

When starting Software Funnels, our software management portal software, we went through this process. Here is our one-sentence statement:

"Software Funnels will exist in order to help entrepreneurs develop, launch, and maintain any software idea, by offering an all-in-one software management portal that allows them to be more efficient & productive, save time & money, and get to market faster!"

You will notice that we were specific as to who, what and why. Just do your best, and try not to make it overly complicated. When you read it, it should get you motivated and excited! It should immediately bring clarity to your mind and spark your vision of what it can become.

Note: For those of you who are more visual type learners, we actually recorded the brainstorming meeting where we came up with our why statement for Software Funnels. It's completely unscripted so you can see firsthand how it's done.

Go to www.SoftwareSecrets.com/training to learn more.

Step 2 - Buy a Domain Name

Now that you've had your brainstorming session, and you've answered several difficult questions about your new software, it's time to use that information to help you find the perfect domain name. We can't stress how important this is. For software, the domain name is the brand and it makes a big difference in your overall success.

This process of choosing a domain name can take several hours of research, and you'll probably end up with a few viable options. Once you feel good about a particular domain name, you should move forward.

When you sit down to research domain names, we recommend that you follow these suggestions:

- **Use your new 'why' statement to help you.** This can spark ideas and point you in the right direction.
- **Research your competition.** A lot of times your competitors' names already have traction in the marketplace. If you can find a similar name, then you can leverage some of their reputation. Just be careful not to directly copy it or make it confusingly similar.
- **Try to explain the purpose of your software in the name.** The closer the name can be to describing the purpose of your software, the better.

- **Keep it short.** Nobody wants to type in a big, long domain name. The shorter, the better.

- **Make it memorable or unique.** If you can't get the exact name, then add something to spice it up. For example, when we were trying to find a name for our live chat and support ticketing software, we couldn't find a name to save our lives, so we started to add animal names in front of 'support'. Rhino-Support.com was available, so we ran with it. It made the name unique and it stood out.

- **Buy the .com version of the domain name if at all possible.** Even with all the new extensions (for example, .plumber, .software or .io), we believe that people still feel more comfortable and have a much higher trust for sites with the .com extension.

- **Avoid hyphens.** You never want a domain with hyphens. When Scott first started out, he and his dad bought the domain Trust-Guard.com for their first software business, because TrustGuard.com was taken. It took them several years, a legal battle, and over $20,000 to eventually buy the domain without the hyphen. Bottom line, buying domains with hyphens doesn't look professional, and people don't trust them.

- **Go with your gut.** Sometimes you have to go with a name because it's the right one, and you just know it when you see it. In this case, do whatever you need to do to secure the name – within reason, of course.

You can see that we have tried to follow the above suggestions with our domain names.

ShopperApproved.com - It describes the benefit to the end consumer of our customer rating and review services. It's short, memorable, unique, and doesn't have any hyphens.

CustomerRewards.com - It is also short, memorable, and unique, and perfectly describes our service to potential business owners. As a side note, this is probably the best domain name we could have possibly bought in the loyalty rewards space, because it describes the actual industry. When we call up a business and say we're from CustomerRewards.com, the name has instant recognition and credibility without that business knowing anything about our company.

While there are dozens of domain name registrars, we generally use GoDaddy.com, mainly because we've used them forever and manage most of our domains there. If we were to start over again, we would probably go with NameCheap.com. They are an amazing company and are highly recommended – they are also a Shopper Approved client with over one million reviews. Whoever you decide to go with, just stay with that company and keep all your domains in once place so you can easily manage them. You can also download domain name apps so that when you are out and about and you get an idea for a domain name, you can quickly check to see if it's available.

The cost to purchase a domain name for a year generally ranges between $4.99 to $11.99. When you first get started, don't be surprised to find that many of the good domain names you want are already taken. That is okay, just keep digging.

If you find a domain that you love, go to the site and see if there's anything there. If not, then the owner of the domain name is likely just parking it, which means there's a good chance it's for sale. We have bought most of our domains from other people that had already registered them. Sometimes we've paid a premium price for them, but other times we've got a steal of a deal. Remember to always start low, and then work towards a middle ground. Most people are willing to negotiate quite a bit just to offload the name and make some quick cash.

Here are some examples of premium pricing we've paid to purchase domain names:

ShopperApproved.com - $2,500
CustomerRewards.com - $15,000
CartRocket.com - $800
TrustGuard.com - $20,000
SoftwareSecrets.com - $4,000

Did your left arm just go a bit numb? A slight pain in your chest?

Sometimes it's really hard to bite the bullet and pay thousands of dollars for a domain name, but having the right name is so important that we are willing to do it.

Don't worry, you will probably get lucky and find your dream domain name for under 10 bucks, but if not, don't hesitate to contact the owner and make an offer. You could even get creative if you're low on funds and ask if you could do a 'lease to buy' option or make payments over time.

Once you do find a solid name that you love and it's available, make sure to do a basic trademark search, just to make sure that no one else already has that name trademarked in your space. Go to tess2.uspto. gov and then click on the link that says 'Basic Word Mark Search'. Look to see if any trademarks are active, and then click on them to see if they are going to be an issue or not. If there are any active trademarks that you feel may be cause for concern, you may want reach out to a trademark lawyer before pulling the trigger on the domain name.

Step 3 - Design Your Logo

Now that you have your domain name, it is time to design your logo.

Yes, your logo.

No, we're not crazy - there's a method to our madness. In our opinion, you'd be crazy to skip this step.

The reason it's important for you to design a logo this early in the process is that having a logo gives you direction, allows you to have something visual to start building from, and gets your creative juices flowing.

It's a psychological phenomenon that we can't explain, but there is real value in creating the logo first.

Duke, our in-house designer, has designed most of our logos. He is amazing. You probably won't have a Duke on your team at first, but that's okay. Thanks to the internet, there are many ways to get access to incredibly talented graphic designers with just a few mouse clicks.

Here are some resources where you can find a great graphic designer for your logo:

- **99designs.com / designcrowd.com** - You get access to a pool of potentially hundreds of designers that all design you a logo, and you pick the one you like the best. The higher prize value you give, the more designers you will get to participate. It's like having a giant team of expert graphic designers all working for you, but you only have to pay the best one.

- **Fiverr.com** - You can hire someone to design a logo for you for as little as 5 bucks, but be careful with this one, because you often get what you pay for (although sometimes you can get lucky). If you decide to go this route, we recommend this resource - www.SoftwareSecrets.com/fiverr. (Note: This is not an affiliate link - we just added this URL in case the resource we recommend changes.)

- **Upwork.com / Guru.com** - These are both sites with networks of thousands of freelance workers; from programmers to designers to copywriters. Simply post your project (i.e. designing a logo), and designers will bid on your project. If you go this route, make sure you look through their portfolios and see what they've designed in the past.

We've used all these companies at different times and for different projects. Here are some pointers to help you succeed while working on your logo with your designer:

- **Ask for unlimited revisions.** This allows you the freedom to make tiny tweaks and changes to your logo until until you're happy.

- **Ask for multiple versions.** Ask the designer to create at least three completely different mockups at first, so you get a variety to choose from.

- **Keep your logo simple.** The more simple your logo is, the better.

- **Add an icon to your logo.** It's good to have a visual anchor that people can remember and relate to when they see your logo. For example, in our Shopper Approved logo, it's a shopping cart with a checkmark in it; in our Rhino Support logo, it's a text box with a rhino horn in it; and in our Customer Rewards logo, it's a gift box with a bow that has the subtle 'CR' in it.

- **Don't settle.** If one designer isn't doing exactly what you want, find another one. Your logo is too important for you to not absolutely love it. It will ultimately determine the direction of your brand.

To give you an idea of what we do and how many versions we go through to find the right look, here's a graphic we made that shows the evolution of our CustomerRewards.com logo:

Concept Sketches & Mockups

Final Logo Design

(You can see a larger, color version if you go to
www.SoftwareSecrets.com/logo)

Note: Once you have a final version of your logo, it doesn't mean that you can't change it in the future. We have changed all of our logos over time, but they never stray too much from the original design. Usually, we just do minor updates to keep them current.

Step 4 - Setup Your Software Funnels Account

Right now you're so early in the software process that this step should only take you a few minutes, but trust us when we tell you that your ultimate success absolutely depends on it. There are so many solutions online that help with project management, that you could literally spend days researching everything available.

But here's the reality. There are no project management tools that exist that will help you to effectively build and manage your software project like Software Funnels can. Before we created Software Funnels, we used 8 completely different 3rd party tools to develop software, and it was an absolute nightmare. We used to have to run separate instances of each tool, create separate accounts, add separate users, and switch back and forth between all the tools constantly to see what was happening at any given time.

But that's all in the past...

The following graphic shows all 8 categories of tools that we actively use to develop and run software, along with some of the software solutions currently on the market for each of those categories:

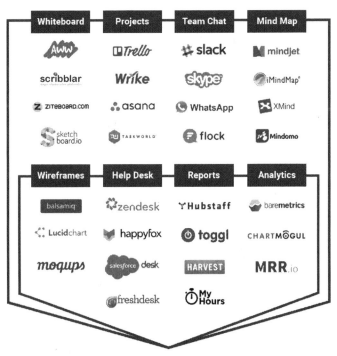

With Software Funnels, ALL of these tools are available in one simple web interface, they all talk to each other, and when you create a user, that user is instantly added to all the tools that you want them to be added to. Bottom line, Software Funnels makes building and managing software development a breeze, and will be one of the main keys to your success.

Now, keep in mind that you don't have to use Software Funnels. You can still be successful using these tools independently of each other, but just know that your project will be a lot more difficult to manage, and it will end up costing you more money and frustration in the long run.

If you recall, in Chapter 2, we taught that one of the best types of software solutions you can create is software that solves your own problem. Well, we built Software Funnels to solve our own problem, and it has fundamentally changed the way we build software.

Note: Because Software Funnels is such an integral part of our software development process, we will be referring to the tools inside of it throughout the remainder of the book, but if you choose not to use Software Funnels, that's okay, the same principles still apply to whatever related 3rd party tool you decide to use.

Step 5 - Brainstorm and Mind Map

Brainstorming and mind mapping officially mark the starting point of your actual software development process.

For optimal results, we suggest that you either get in front of an actual whiteboard, or use the 'Whiteboard' tool in Software Funnels to come up with your rough high-level outline, then use the 'Mind Maps' tool to organize your thoughts and map out your overall software structure.

These are important steps, which you will frequently refer back to and adjust over time.

In our Software Secrets Training System we go into more detail regarding brainstorming and mind mapping. We even recorded several of our brainstorming meetings for you to watch, so if you're a member of our training system, refer to the brainstorming and mind mapping module.

Breaking it down

Let's begin by breaking this down into two bite-sized chunks.

We're going to start on a higher level with the user structure, then we'll drill down into the user interface.

First Step - User Structure:

Your first item of business is to brainstorm and mind map the 'User Structure' for your software.

The user structure is all about who will be using your software, and how they will be using it in relation to your backend control panel/portal.

To determine the user structure, ask yourself questions like:

- Who will be using or will need access to the software? (This will likely be you, the 'Admin', along with other potential users like your staff, your clients, your client's customers, affiliates, sales agents, partners, etc.) Write these down in a list.
- How many backend portals will you need in order to satisfy the needs of each type of user? (For example, you as an admin, will likely have a completely different set of tools in your user portal than a client would.) Keep in mind that different types of users can share the same portal. For example, admin and staff can probably access the same admin portal, but staff might just have fewer features available.

■ What unique areas or functions do each of these users need access to in their individual portals in order to perform their proper functions? (These could be things like settings or preferences, billing, statistics, dashboard, etc.)

Writing these things out on a whiteboard first is ideal because things are going to be messy when you first start. Just know that there's really no right or wrong way to do this. The most important thing is to just get everything out of your brain - draw boxes, arrows, circles, make lists, highlight and underline - whatever you need to do to start creating structure around each type of user.

When we started building Customer Rewards, we brainstormed our user structure on a whiteboard, and we ultimately came up with five different types of users, which were; Admin, Project Managers, Sales Agents, Clients, and Client's Customers. We came up with this particular list because of our business model.

■ We needed an Admin section so that we could have access to all of the high-level reports (clients, client statistics, financials, etc.).

■ We needed a Project Manager section because each of our clients were going to be assigned a Project Manager, and they had to have access to all of their specific client's information.

■ We needed a Sales Agents section so that our sales agents could enter new sales into the system, charge their credit cards, and have access to certain limited client information.

■ We needed a Clients area where the client could log into their control panel and have access to the actual software tools, and a list of their particular customers.

■ And finally, we needed a Client's Customers area where our client's customers could login to see their customer rewards and reward status, and redeem their points.

Now, when it came to backend portals, ultimately we only needed three. One for Admin, Project Managers, and Sales Agents, one for Clients, and one for our Client's Customers.

With this basic, high-level information we created our first mind map, which looked like this:

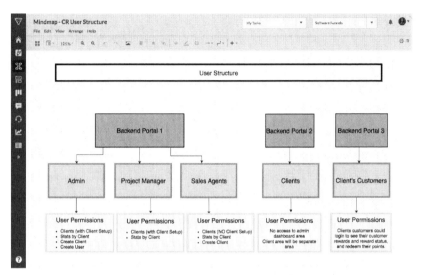

(You can see a larger, color version if you go to www.softwaresecrets.com/mind-map)

Ultimately, you can use mind maps to map out anything you can imagine. Mind maps really help to organize your thoughts in a constructive, organized way so that you can better understand how the different parts all work together.

Second Step - User Interface:

Once you have the user structure outlined, the next step is to brainstorm and map out the 'User Interface' (also referred to as UI).

The user interface is basically where you put yourself in the shoes of each user and then walk through your backend control panel (the area that the user logs into), to determine which tools and pages that they will need access to.

The easiest way to do this is to break out each your backend portals individually, and then go through each one and just write down all of the pages that you can think of that the highest level user would have access to if they logged in. (Don't worry about any users with lower permissions right now, because you can always remove or hide tools and features from them later.)

Some examples of pages may include:

- Dashboard pages
- Setup pages
- Settings/preference pages
- Analytics/stats pages
- Tool pages (these are pages that are directly related to your software)
- Billing pages
- Client stats pages

As you're reviewing all of your pages, keep in mind that you will probably miss some on the first round. This is perfectly fine. The important thing is to just brainstorm and get things down. Don't let the pursuit of perfection paralyze you into doing nothing. Over time, any pages that you may have missed will become obvious, and you can add them in at that point.

Going back to our Customer Rewards example, here is an example of what our Admin portal user interface would include:

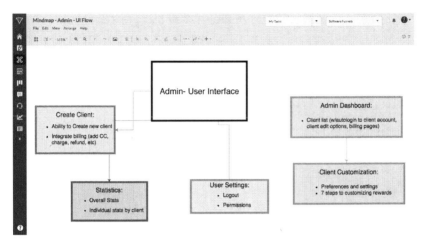

*(You can see a larger, color version if you go to
www.SoftwareSecrets.com/admin-map)*

We go through this process for each portal. If you were to put all of
your portals into one mind map, like we did with Customer Rewards,
you would have a master mind map that looks something like this:

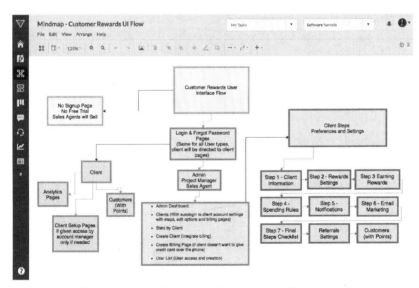

*(You can see a larger, color version if you go to
www.SoftwareSecrets.com/portals)*

It's not necessary to have a master mind map, but it does give you the ability to see the entire user interface at once, which can help you see gaps and add or remove options that you may or may not need as the project progresses over time. Mind maps should be living documents.

Step 6 - Wireframe Mockups for Your Designer

Now that you have listed out all the pages you believe you will need, it is time to wireframe each one out as a mockup for the designer.

Here are the steps we take to wireframe a page.

First Step - Super Rough Draft:

Open a new Whiteboard on Software Funnels, or get a piece of paper and pretend it is the webpage you're going to design. Then draw everything that needs to be on that page. Sometimes when we're doing this, we'll mess up and redraw a page two or three times, or we'll scratch things out. This step is meant to be very quick and messy, and to just give you a starting point.

Here is an example of a rough draft we made for one of the pages on CustomerRewards.com:

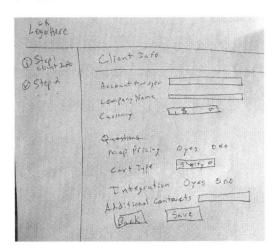

(You can see a larger version if you go to www.SoftwareSecrets. com/mockup)

As you can see, our rough drafts are about as quick and messy as you can get, but they give us something that we can build on. You need to create one of these for every single page in each portal of your user interface.

Second Step - Wireframe:

Next, take one of your rough drafts and create a wireframe using the Wireframe tool in Software Funnels to create a nicer version of your rough draft.

Here's an example of turning the rough draft we just referenced into an actual wireframe. It's not pretty but it makes a huge difference in the design process:

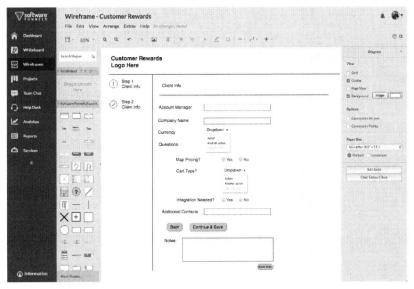

(You can see a larger, color version if you go to www.SoftwareSecrets.com/wireframe)

Also, here is a short video of how we actually created the wireframe using the Wireframe tool in Software Funnels:
www.SoftwareSecrets.com/wireframe-video

Typically, wireframes will take you a bit longer than the rough draft, but it should still be relatively fast. You're not looking to create the Mona Lisa here. Wireframes just need to have enough information on them so that when you send them to the graphic designer, they have a good idea of how to design the page.

Tip: As you begin to wireframe all the pages that you came up with in Step 5, one way you can significantly speed up the process is to create a wireframe 'template' that includes the header, menu, and footer. Once the template is done, you just load it up and fill in the middle portion of each page. This can easily be done with the Wireframe tool in Software Funnels.

Step 7 - Hire a Graphic Designer

When building software it is absolutely vital that you find a great designer. The look and feel of your website is incredibly important, and makes a huge impression on your prospects and how they relate to your brand.

Earlier, in 'Step 3 - Design Your Logo', we mentioned that we have a full-time in-house designer, but when you're first starting out, you don't need a full-time designer on your team. You just need someone that can design all of the backend user interface pages on a per hour or per project basis, and eventually help you with the front end pages (when you get closer to launching your software).

You may be wondering what this is going to cost. The truth is, we don't know the scope of your specific project, so we can't tell you exactly, but here are some estimates for a simple SAAS product.

Home page and front end / marketing pages ~ 40 hours
Backend user interface pages ~ 4 hours per page

So let's say your software service has around 15 backend web pages, and you have a one-page home page for your marketing. Then let's say you find a designer at a rate of $30/hour. That means you could estimate around $3,000 in design costs. Keep in mind that these are just estimates.

Can you find designers at $5-$10/hour? Sure you can, but we have found through many bad experiences, that the cheaper the designer, the poorer the quality. The key is to do your research and find someone with a great portfolio that can work with your vision. In the grand scheme of things, $30/hr for a graphic designer is well worth it – especially if they are properly managed and they stay on task.

How to Find a Graphic Designer

If the designer that created your logo in Step 3 did a great job and was easy to work with, then this is where you should start. Reach out to that person and see if they would be interested in working with you on an ongoing basis to help you design the X number of pages you need to get started. Find out what hourly rate they will charge. If it fits in your budget, then you should be good to go.

We highly suggest that you just hire them to do one of the pages first so that if they don't design to the quality you would like, then you aren't locked into them for all the remaining pages.

If you don't want to use the designer that did your logo, then you need to find someone you can work with. Here are some places to start:

- Upwork.com
- Guru.com
- Local universities or design schools
- Our Graphic Designers - In addition to our in-house designer, we have a handful of talented 3rd party graphic design companies that we work with. If you've signed up for our Software Secrets Training System, we actually give you direct access to the same design companies that we use. And as a Software Secrets member, you pay the exact same rates that we pay, even with our higher volume. To sign up for our training system, go to www.SoftwareSecrets.com/training.

When posting your project, make sure you are specific in what you are looking for. Here are some things you should include in your project description:

- You need only one page designed for this first project, but if you are happy with the work, you will hire them for your remaining design needs.
- You are looking for someone who designs in any of the Adobe creative suite products, preferably Photoshop.
- You are looking for someone with User Interface (UI) design experience.
- Also, you are looking for someone with SAAS (or the type of software you are creating) design experience.
- Ask them to give you a link to their portfolio of recent work that is related to what you are looking for.
- You expect to get the mockup one-page design back within a 48-hour period from when they are hired.

Make sure that you send them your wireframe, your logo and your color scheme so they can use them as inspiration. Also, at this point, the page you send them should be a backend page - most likely a dashboard page. You want to design the entire backend first before you even think about the front end. In fact, your home page and any other front end pages should be the last thing you design, (we discuss this in more detail in chapter 7).

Usually, if you're not blown away by a designer's initial one-page design, then that's a really good sign that you need to hire a different designer. Yes, you might be out a little bit of money, but it will save you a lot of pain and frustration in the long run.

Step 8 - Design Pages

Once your designer has completed the first backend page, and has created a look and feel that you really like, use that as a template and start sending them more wireframes.

Keep in mind that you don't have to wait for all the pages to be wireframed before you start designing. Many times, we send wireframes one by one as we get them done. We recommend using the 'Projects' tool in Software Funnels to effectively manage the designs with your designer. (We discuss Project Management in much more detail later in the book.)

As your designer completes each page, they will save them as some type of vector file. Our in-house designer designs everything in Adobe Photoshop, and then saves all the files in Photoshop's default .psd format, and also as a .jpg file for us to view.

In Step 6, we showed you an example of a rough draft and a wireframed page. Here is an example of that same page as completed design from our designer:

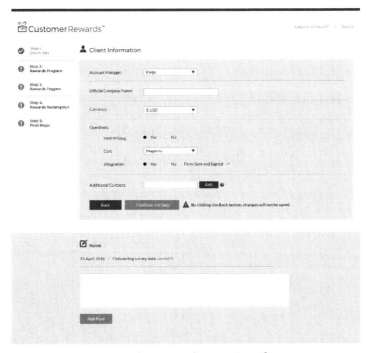

(You can see a larger, color version if you go to www.SoftwareSecrets.com/design)

As you can see, it's quite different from the piece of paper we drew at the beginning, but hopefully it helps you to see just how vital it is to have the design done first.

It's also important to know that we didn't accept the first design the designer sent over for review. We made multiple changes until it was exactly how we wanted it. Remember not to sign off on the design until you are completely happy. You also may have noticed that we changed the logo after this design page was created. It just goes to show that you can always change things as time goes on.

Step 9 - Hire Programmers

Hiring programmers is one of the most important steps, because who you choose to build out your idea and turn it into a reality can literally make or break your business.

Although we've been fortunate over the years to be able to work with a lot of great programmers, not all of them worked out. In fact, we've had to scrap projects in the past because of bad programmers, and it's cost us a lot of wasted time and money. These days, thanks to our 12 Step process, we are able to greatly improve the quality of the programmers we work with, and it's made a huge difference.

In this step, our goal is to help you to hire amazing programmers, so that you have the best possible opportunities for success.

Different programming languages
First you need to realize that there are several different programming languages. Here are some of the most used programming languages for SAAS:

- Javascript
- PHP

- .NET
- Ruby/Rails
- Python
- Node
- Meteor.js
- Java

Except for Software Funnels, we've built all of our other software products using PHP and Javascript, because we find they are the easiest languages to find good programmers for. These programming languages are also free and widely used.

Sometimes you might need to use a specific programming language when building a certain type of software solution. Whatever the language is, it doesn't really matter as long as you find an amazing developer that knows that language and can get the job done.

When we started building Software Funnels, in order to accelerate our development process, we used some open source solutions that were programmed in languages we didn't even know existed until we started to integrate them. But it really didn't matter to us what the languages were. We just found great programmers that knew each language, and we were able to move forward without skipping a beat.

Once you decide what language you're going to use, it's time to create your programming hierarchy and start looking for some rockstar programmers.

Your Programming Hierarchy
Here is what we suggest that the hierarchy should look like for your initial programming team:

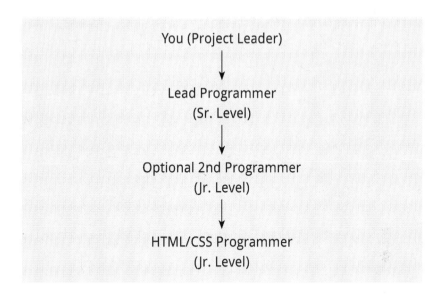

When you're first starting your project, it may be tempting to hire several programmers right away so that you can get done faster, but from our experience, that's not the best idea.

Ideally, you want to start with a small team of no more than 3 programmers. You want a Senior or Lead Programmer, a Junior Programmer (optional), and a part-time HTML/CSS programmer.

The main reason why you want to start with a small team is because the more programmers you add at the beginning, the harder it becomes to effectively manage and communicate with them. Before you can scale, you need to learn how to be an effective project manager and how to effectively communicate with your programmers; whether US-based or overseas. (Later in the book, we teach you how to effectively manage and communicate with your team.)

If you can afford two full-time programmers, then that's fine, but you must be very careful how you go about it. One of the programmers needs to be the lead, and the other needs to be the junior programmer that follows the lead. You, as the project leader, will have to be very clear on how the two work together so that money and time are not wasted.

Where to Hire Programmers

It's now time to begin your talent search, but where do you go to find the best talent? Where do you find the rock stars that will ultimately become a key part of your dream team?

Here's where we suggest you start your job search:

- Upwork.com
- Guru.com
- Freelancer.com
- Our Programming Teams - If you're a Software Secrets member, you get direct access to the same amazing programming company that we use to build our software, at the same low rates that we pay. And the best part is that these programmers are already trained on how we build software, so you can hit the ground running. To sign up for our training program, go to www.SoftwareSecrets.com/training.

The secret to finding a good programmer

If you're going to use a freelance site like Upwork, Guru, or Freelancer to hire your programmers, post a small test project, find two or three of the most promising programmers, and hire all of them. Give each one the same programming project - something that they should be able to complete in less than eight hours. This process allows you to see who is dedicated to the project, and who is willing to ask questions and communicate (which is very important). It also gives you the ability to see them in action and see who delivers the best final result. It's a little more expensive initially, but you will find out very quickly who you like working with the best and who really stands out.

Here is what to include in your job post:

1. Type of programming language you want to code in (e.g. PHP, Javascript)

2. Tell them you are looking for a senior programmer with at least three years experience

3. You want at least two references in their bid or resume

4. Give them the small project you want them to accomplish in detail (you need to give specific details of the small task you want them to do and give them a deadline to finish the task)

5. Tell them they must finish the project within 24 hours of hiring them but the actual work cannot take more than eight hours

6. If possible, pay them an hourly wage instead of a one-time fee for the project, so you can determine what their hourly rate will be after the test is completed

You need to follow this hiring process for both the lead programmer, the Jr. level programmer, and the HTML/CSS programmer.

While the programmers are working on the test project, you need to pay close attention to how each one did, and consider who you liked working with the best? Who did the best work? Who hit their deadlines? Who communicated the best?

By this point you should know who you want to work with and who you want on your team. If none of the three did a good job, and you wouldn't like working with any of them, then run the ad or job post again and start over with another three until you find the best fit for you and your project.

When you do find the right person, make sure you clearly set your expectations:

- What hours do you want them working? (If they're overseas, we recommend that you have them work a shift where there are at least a few hours of overlap where you're both working. For example, we have our Pakistan team work a swing shift. This allows us to have about 3 hours of overlap each morning so that we can discuss what they worked on, and also have time to troubleshoot together as needed.)

- Will they be working full-time for you? (We highly recommend that you hire your lead and Jr. programmers full-time if possible and your HTML/CSS programmer on a per-project hourly basis.)

- What type of reporting do you want from them on a daily basis? (We go into this a bit more in the project management chapter, but we recommend that they send you a report every day of what they worked on and what percentage of completion they're at on each task. If you use Software Funnels, the 'Reports' tool tracks all of this for you.)

Paying your programmers

We highly suggest you pay your programmers by the hour and not by the project. Just trust us on this. We also highly recommend that you avoid trading equity or ownership for programming time.

You may want to go back and read the 'Trading Equity or Ownership for Startup Help' section in Chapter 3.

Another thing you need to make absolutely sure of, is that your full-time programmers are working only for you and that they will not be freelancing anymore. The best way to ensure this is to give them a good hourly wage, anywhere from $20-25/hr for a lead developer, and around $15-$20/hr for a junior programmer or HTML/CSS developer. Now, you can get programmers cheaper than this, but quality and experience come with a higher price, and are more than worth the extra money.

For some of our larger, more established companies, we hire local programmers that live here in Utah, whom we pay significantly more than our overseas programmers. However, whenever we start a new company, we use overseas programmers that live in Pakistan, India and the Philippines. We always pay them higher than normal wages for those countries, which has paid off tremendously. They are all incredibly loyal and very hard workers.

If you do end up trying to save money and find a programmer at $10-15/hr, then make sure they are amazing and are only working for you. The worst thing that can happen is that three months into the project they find another client who will pay them $20/hr and now you're up a creek without a paddle.

There are US-based programmers who expect to make high five or even six figures. We suggest you avoid those types of programmers when starting out. Having developed a lot of software, we've found that there's really no need for someone at that level when you're in the early stages. Those higher-end programmers definitely have their place, but in our opinion, when starting out you really just need a workhorse who will follow basic instructions and get things done. Also, you probably won't have the budget for that level of programmer starting out.

What If I am a Programmer?

As we've mentioned previously, we are not programmers. In fact, neither of us have ever written a single line of code, and if we did, we would probably destroy the entire company! Ironically, we feel that this is to our advantage, because it's forced us to let the programmers we've hired do the heavy lifting, while we've focused our time on vision, design and architecture and marketing.

If you are a programmer, you will have a lot of leverage and insight that we didn't necessarily have when starting out, but there may be some pitfalls in the long run. The biggest issue you have to be careful of is getting so deep into the programming that you don't focus on the other vital aspects of the business. The key to a successful company is to get to the point where you are actively working *on* your business, and not *in* your business, as quickly as humanly possible.

Here's what we mean.

Logic assumes that if you're a programmer, then your time and focus should be spent programming. If that is the case, then who is going to do everything else? Who is going to do the mock-ups and the wireframing? Who is going to work with the graphic designer? Who is going to manage the billing, the marketing, the partnerships and the sales? Yes, you can program and do everything else, but you will get quickly overwhelmed and ultimately get very little done.

What you really need to spend your time on is being the architect and project leader so that you can see the full picture and orchestrate the moving pieces. If you are always head down in code, it will be very hard to build the software in a timely manner – especially once you start selling it and want to scale in any meaningful way.

Our advice would be to hire a programmer and be the project leader/manager. If you are a programmer, you will be able to explain very well what you want, and you can easily troubleshoot or explain things to the programmer that they're not understanding. This will allow you to accelerate your development time considerably.

Again, this is our opinion. Can you make things work if you're the programmer? Sure. Will it be successful? Sure, but it will be a lot slower. We've seen this happen first hand with friends and family who are programmers.

If, however, you do decide to be the main programmer, then here are some suggestions for you:

1. **Separate your roles.** In order to be both the project leader and the programmer, you have to make sure that you dedicate

separate time to both roles. It may even be a good idea to plan specific times of the day when you put on the project leader/manager hat.

2. **Project manage yourself.** In conjunction with 1. above, try to treat yourself like an employee that is being hired by your company, and use a project management system like the Projects and Reports tools in Software Funnels to manage yourself. This will help you to stay on track and will also make it easy for you to add additional team members when you need them.

3. **Make yourself replaceable.** Build your software so that another programmer can come in and take your place without too much hassle. This will make it easier for you to transition out of programming when the time comes for you to become the project leader full-time.

4. **Get outside opinions regularly.** Often times, programmers can become so involved in creating code that they start to lose vision. Asking for outside help and opinions can really help you to keep seeing the bigger picture.

Step 10 - HTML/CSS Development

Once you start getting designs back from the graphic designer, and you officially sign off on them, it's time to start sending them one by one to the HTML/CSS programmer that you've hired. (Note: If you want to send all the page designs at once, then that is fine too, but it might take longer before you can start programming.)

At this point, all you need is the HTML/CSS for the pages in order to turn them into actual web pages that the programmers can work with. Tell your HTML/CSS programmer that you do not need any functionality or programming. You simply need the HTML/CSS files for each page.

The reason why you need an HTML/CSS programmer is because you don't want the lead programmer worrying about all the HTML/ CSS. Typically, lead programmers are not proficient in HTML/CSS, so having them do it will just create a big bottleneck and slow development to a crawl. HTML/CSS programmers are specialized and can do their job independently of the lead programmer.

One thing you will need to decide at this point is what pages you want to be 'responsive', which is another word for websites that are tablet and mobile friendly. A responsive page flexes and changes its shape and look based on the size of the screen the page is viewed on. Generally, to start out we don't make any of our admin pages responsive, but we do consider making any backend pages responsive that the customer will see or access regularly, so they look good on any device the customer views them on. This process takes extra time and money, so it is totally up to you, especially when it comes to the backend, but keep in mind that all front end marketing pages are expected to all be responsive nowadays.

Once each page has been developed into HTML/CSS, have the HTML/CSS programmer upload them to a server, if possible, so that you can see each page live on a web browser, and check the look and functionality on tablets and phones to make sure that everything looks right.

A tool that we use to test our pages on all the different browser types is Browserstack.com. This service is totally worth the small monthly fee, because it allows you to test how your site looks and feels on every type of operating system, browser and mobile device.

Once you have approved all backend pages, have the programmer send you all the files so you have a backup copy. (We highly recommend that you manage the entire HTML/CSS process in your 'Projects' tab if you're using Software Funnels.)

Step 11 - Hosting and Servers

Now it's time to get some hosting for your software. We've made a lot of mistakes with this step over the years, so please pay close attention.

The truth is that you don't need anything fancy or big starting out, because, more than likely, you and your programming team will be the only people on your site. However, just because you don't need a large server or hosting service, that doesn't mean you don't need high quality.

When choosing a hosting service, you want to look for something flexible and scalable so that you can simply allocate additional resources when needed, instead of running out of space and having to migrate servers, which is a huge pain. You also want to look for a hosting service that allows you to have a dedicated server, or a dedicated server instance that gives you the features of a dedicated server so you can control all aspects of the server.

When we were first starting out, we thought we could just get a simple $5 or $10/mo hosting service and we'd be fine. What ended up happening is that we grew so fast that our hosting couldn't keep up with our growth and we ran into multiple issues with disk space, databases and bandwidth - all of which could have been easily avoided if we had had some foresight.

As you can imagine, these issues were the cause of many stressful days and sleepless nights trying to get our hosting services back up and running whenever our website would crash or unexpectedly slow down because our hosting wasn't robust enough. In fact, if we were to rate the #1 most stressful problem with running a software company, hosting and servers would have to be the winner.

Fortunately, these days, we have a lot fewer issues with servers. We either buy huge dedicated servers that we host and manage ourselves at a nearby datacenter for our larger companies, or we host with Amazon for our new and growing companies. For the purposes of this book, we will focus on Amazon Web Services (AWS). Specifically, we use Amazon EC2 servers. We also run a lot of our images and files on Amazon S3 or Cloudfront.

We use and recommend Amazon because they are huge, and the services they offer to web developers are the same services they run their own systems on, so you know they are both high end and ultra dependable. Some extremely large companies run on their servers, like Netflix, Airbnb, Yelp, and Pinterest, just to name a few. Security, global infrastructure, speed, and infinite scalability are just a few more of the many reasons to go with them. But one of the best reasons to go with Amazon is that you can start for around $25/month and can scale infinitely on demand.

Infinite scalability means that once your site is uploaded and running, you don't have to worry about migrating to another host or service provider because you've run out of space. This seems silly if you're just starting out, but we've had to migrate our sites and databases several times over the years, and each migration was incredibly stressful and nerve-racking. To put this into perspective, migrating servers is like having major surgery - the doctors say that you have a good chance of making it, but there are a lot of unexpected things that can go wrong, and you could end up dead. So, it's best to try to avoid it if at all possible.

All this talk about hosting and servers might sound a bit overwhelming at this point. But don't worry; it is something that you can easily hand over to an expert.

Setting up your Server

Funny enough, we have no idea how to setup a server with Amazon. The truth is that setting up a server with Amazon is quite complicated, and it takes someone who knows what they are doing.

The first time we did it, we simply went to Upwork.com and created a job post that said that we needed a server administrator with expertise in Amazon EC2 to set up an Amazon EC2 server for us. We also needed them to help us understand anything else to get it all set up and hooked to our domain name. We paid around $300 to get this all done and it was worth every penny.

When you do hire this person, make sure that you have them set up two server instances; one called 'Live' and the other called 'Dev' (short for development). Have them point the live server to live.yourdomainname.com, and the dev server to dev.yourdomainname.com.

Here are some alternatives if you don't want to go the Amazon route:

Rackspace.com - this is a very reputable company that has the infrastructure and resources to help you succeed, but it comes at a price.

A2hosting.com - they are not as scalable as Amazon, but they are a great company and will go out of their way to help you. They are also a lot cheaper than Rackspace.

Setting up Cloudflare

The next thing you want to do once your server is up and running is to set up a CloudFlare.com account. CloudFlare is a software service that automatically keeps all the viruses and spammy traffic from ever reaching your server. It also caches or saves a copy of your website, and automatically displays it if your server ever goes down or has any issues.

We use CloudFlare for all our websites, and we highly recommend you use it as well. You can use the free version when starting out, and then pay for the Pro or Business plan once you launch and really start growing. Your Lead programmer can most likely get you all set up with CloudFlare so that it is hooked to your domain name (via your DNS settings), and is pointing to your server correctly.

(If you're a member of the Software Secrets Training System, you get access to all our videos and training modules, where we go deeper into setting up your server and infrastructure properly. We also give you access to the same Server Administrator that we use, so everything gets set up correctly.)

Step 12 - Create an Opt-In Page

Now that you have your domain name, logo, hosting, designer and programmers in place, it is time to get your feet wet with your very first public-facing web page. This first page should be an opt-in page and will give you the ability to get some initial content on your domain name that may help for future SEO (Search Engine Optimization) efforts. It also allows you to collect emails from people that may be interested in your future product/service that you can market to later on.

We highly recommend you use ClickFunnels.com to set up your opt-in page. The main reason is that you can have an amazing-looking page up within 20 minutes or less.

Do not spend a lot of time on this. For now, you just need a basic headline, some teaser text, and a way for the user to enter their email address. ClickFunnels makes this quick and painless, and their team is great if you need any help.

Here is an example of the opt-in page we created for SoftwareFunnels.com using ClickFunnels

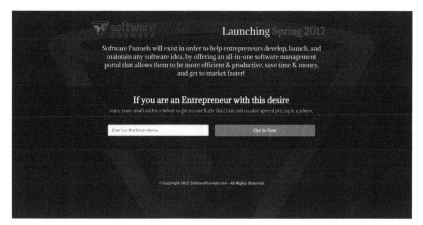

(You can see a larger, color version if you go to www.SoftwareSecrets.com/optin)

Are We Done Yet?

At this point your head probably feels like it's going to explode. We never said it would be easy to create a software empire, but it will definitely be worth it if you can stay engaged and follow through.

Remember that it's okay to make mistakes, mess things up, and even miss things. Even if you follow our advice to the letter, there is still a learning curve involved. Through the entire process you will make many stressful, difficult and challenging decisions. This is to be expected and is perfectly normal. The important thing is to keep putting one foot in front of the other – keep moving forward, even when things are hard. Anyone that was ever successful always pushed through when things were tough, and they all struggled at what they were doing when they first started, but they got better and better.

Also keep in mind that software is a continual work in progress – it will never be finished. But if you continue to put your heart and soul into it over time, it will evolve into something truly amazing, and change your life and the lives of thousands of others. If you had seen some of our software products when they first launched, you would have laughed out loud because they were so bad. But we continued to develop and improve them over time, and now they make millions.

Follow these steps and you will be well on your way to building something truly amazing.

CHAPTER 5

Project Management 101

I f you have completed steps one through twelve, it is now time to move forward with the actual development of your software. It may feel like a long time coming, but if you've properly laid your foundation by following the steps we've outlined, the programming process is going to be much more enjoyable, and a lot smoother.

If you haven't finished the 12 steps, then we highly recommend that you go back and review them, and do your best to implement them before you move on to the programming process.

Goal Setting

It is very important that you set goals and milestones for yourself and for your team before you get started. The truth is that there are thousands of goal setting articles and books out there, so we aren't going to rewrite what has already been said, but we do want to give you some tips and strategies that have helped us.

First, come up with what you believe is a realistic target goal for you to finish the first version (minimum viable product) of your software - where it is ready to be beta tested. The truth is that unless you're a fortune teller and can predict the future, you will have to make the best educated guess based on your situation (i.e. how much time you have to commit, what time or resources you have available, how complicated the software is, how many programmers you plan on having, etc.)

Second, however long you just estimated it will take to complete version 1.0, you need to <u>double</u> it. This tip comes from a lot of experience, and applying it will save you a lot of pain and frustration down the road.

With almost every piece of software we've ever created, the amount of time from inception to beta has usually took double the originally estimated time to complete, and sometimes longer. Rarely does it take less than double the estimated time.

Keep in mind that you should still give your team their timeframes and goals based on your original estimations. This way, you have plenty of leeway if they exceed their development deadlines.

Creating a Timeline

When first starting out, one way that you can quickly estimate your completion date is to break down your development time into chunks. This not only gives you smaller, more attainable goals, but also helps you to visualize major milestones in your project development. Here are the original time chunks that we set when developing one of our recent software projects, CustomerRewards.com:

Customer Rewards Projected Timeline:

30 days - Admin dashboard with client and user creation, sales billing platform (Stripe integration), billing platform.

30 days - Client setup five-step process. This is where the account manager sets up the client's details about their rewards program.

15 days - Client dashboard creation and access, analytics, settings, billing (invoices), etc.

15 days - Customer dashboard creation and access, reward stats

30 days - Magento extension integration, Magento code changes, triggers and hooks.

Once we created this rough timeline, we used the estimates to come up with our original completion goal date, and then we doubled it, making our actual completion time frame eight months.

Once you have your project 'chunks', you can start to break them down into smaller tasks. This is where a project management system becomes invaluable, because without an easy and effective way to manage these tasks, you will get overwhelmed very quickly.

Project Management is one of the most important skills that any software owner can possibly learn.

Your Project Management System

By now you know that we love the 'Projects' tool in Software Funnels, but if you're not a Software Funnels member, and you have a project management system that you really like, then use that instead. You just need something to keep all your tasks in one place; organized and prioritized.

Ultimately, your programming team, whether it be one programmer or many, need to know exactly what they should be working on at all times. You are the captain of the ship, and it is up to you to guide the ship where it needs to go. The programmer's job is to code – not to worry about what to do next.

The following three pages contain screenshots of how we set up our project boards so that we can effectively communicate and manage priorities, and so that our programmers know exactly what they should be working on at all times.

These are the actual screenshots that we send to new programmers that come on board, in order to teach them how to use the 'Projects' tool in Software Funnels.

The first screenshot is an overview of a Project Board, and it explains what each column is inside the board, and how a programmer is supposed to manage each task on the board.

The second screenshot shows how we use Priority labels to show programmers which task to work on first, second and third, along with the rules.

The third screenshot shows what an actual task looks like when you open it, and all of the tools and features that the programmer can use to manage that particular task.

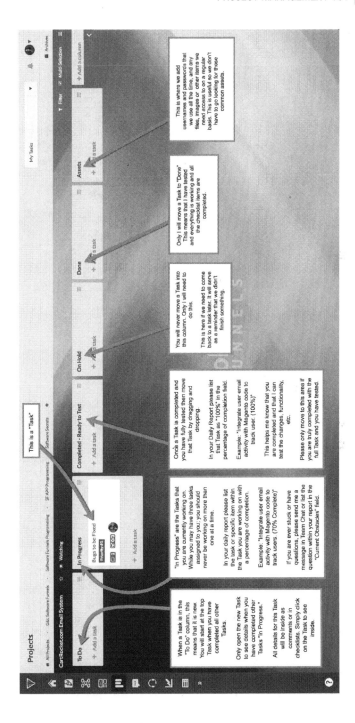

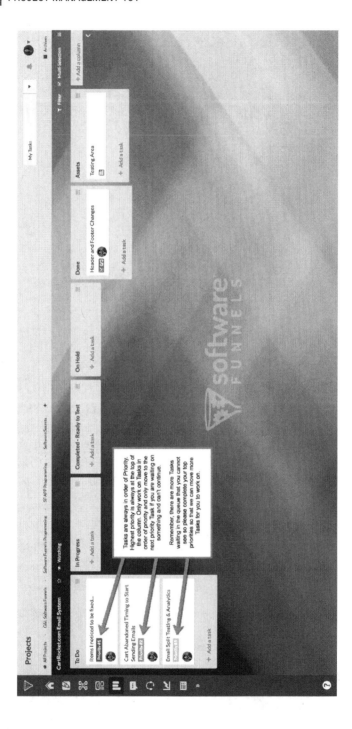

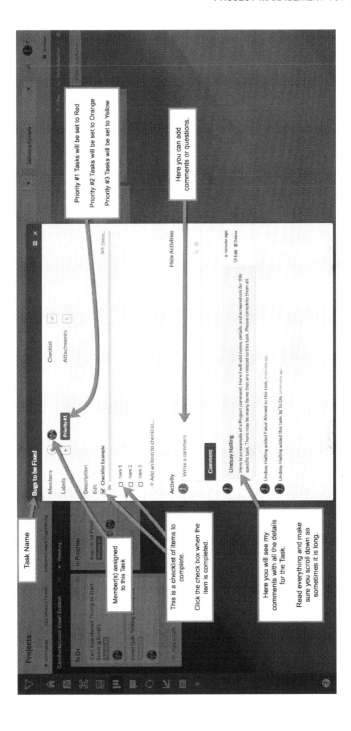

*(You can see a larger, color versions of all three screenshots
if you go to www.SoftwareSecrets.com/projects,
www.SoftwareSecrets.com/priorities, and
www.SoftwareSecrets.com/projects-task)*

Here are some additional tips that have made our programmers
very productive:

▪ **Never give a programmer more than three tasks at a time.**
By nature, programmers are problem solvers, so if you put
more than three tasks in front of them, their big brains are going to try to figure out everything all at once. When they try to
do this, they quickly get overwhelmed, their efficiency goes way
down, and nothing gets done, or at least nothing gets done in
a timely manner.

It's way more effective to feed tasks to them over time, but it
takes a lot of discipline to do this, because there are always
multiple tasks that are constantly fighting for priority. This is
where you come in. You control the priority of the tasks they
work on.

Your job is to always have multiple tasks prioritized and ready
to go in advance, in case your programmers finish the three
tasks they're currently working on faster than you anticipated.
You need your own projects board with all the upcoming tasks
prioritized and ready to go. Make sure that the programmers
do not have access to this board. The key is to only move a new
task onto the programmer's board if they have moved one of
their three current tasks into the 'Completed - Ready to Test'
column.

If you are worried that your programmers will complete all
three of their tasks before you wake up in the morning, you can
add one or two products to the 'To Do' column, but all the rest
of the tasks should be on your hidden board.

■ **Prioritize your programmer's tasks.** Since your programmers should never have more than 3 tasks on their project board at any given time, it's very important to prioritize them from highest to lowest priority.

For example, when we give a programmer a task, we label it with either a red 'Priority #1', an orange 'Priority #2', or a yellow 'Priority #3' label, and we always sort them from #1 to #3, top to bottom. This tells the programmer what the #1 priority is at any given time. Our programmers know that they should always work on priority #1 until it is either done and moved to the 'Completed - Ready to Test' column, or until they get stuck, at which point they can move to priority #2. If they happen to get done all 3 of their tasks before we get online in the morning, (which hardly ever happens) then they know that they should do something productive like review the log files, add comments and documentation to their code, or start on one of the tasks in the 'To Do' column until we get online.

If at any time, Priority #1 changes, then as the project manager, you need to go in and change the labels on all three of their tasks to reflect the new priority hierarchy, and then reach out to the programmer and let them know. Even if they're in the middle of working on a Priority #1 item, if you change that priority, they should immediately stop working on it and start working on the new Priority #1.

You may be thinking that the priority labels are redundant. Well, the truth is that they are; however, it is important to have them psychologically. Just having the projects in order from highest to lowest is not enough. You need to add the labels so that it is 100% clear what they always need to work on first.

■ **Don't give timelines to specific tasks.** When starting out, you should never give a task a timeline. The reason for this is that you really don't know how long it is going to take and the programmer doesn't either. They can estimate, but all it will be is a guess. If a programmer tries to hit an unrealistic timeline, then the code may end up buggy or incomplete.

Just because you think something shouldn't take a long time, that doesn't mean it won't. If something is taking longer than you anticipated, reach out to the programmer, and ask them how that task is going, and if they are stuck or have any specific questions. More than likely you didn't give them enough detail, the task was more involved than you anticipated, or the task created coding changes in other areas that needed to be worked on.

If you're working with your programmers on a daily basis, you will have a very good idea of their capabilities and their work capacity. As long as you are actively involved every day, they will work at their full capacity and you'll get a high ROI with a fast turnaround. However, if you slack off and don't actively manage them on a daily basis, their efficiency will quickly plummet and your project will take a lot longer. If that happens, it's not their fault, it's yours.

■ **Don't move a task to 'Done' until it is actually completed.** As the project manager, you are the master juggler. You have to evaluate all the problems, features or ideas that come up, decide how to deal with them, and prioritize them based on the resources available to you. But <u>priority one, no matter what, is that you focus on the tasks the programmers are currently working on, and that you keep them actively engaged and moving forward</u>. If a specific task is taking too long, then you need to reevaluate the importance of that task and either wait it out, break it down into smaller pieces, cut it out, or put it 'on hold' so that the programmers can keep moving forward.

Communicating With Your Team

It is so important that you keep a direct, open line of communication with your team. This will be easy if your team works in the same office as you, but more than likely your team will be remote.

Your team must know that they can always talk to you, (or the project manager if it's someone else). They need to know the hours that you will be available for communication. They need to feel comfortable that they can ask you questions. In fact, you need to set an expectation that you expect them to ask any and every question they have. A programmer that doesn't ask questions probably isn't the right person.

Surprisingly, proper communication requires the right tools. There are so many tools that you can use to communicate with your team, including email, project management systems, phone, video conferencing, chat and more.

Using Team Chat

We use 'Team Chat' in Software Funnels to communicate with our team every day. 'Team Chat' is probably one of the coolest tools we've ever created, because it allows us to communicate with anyone on our team through multiple channels, depending on what type of communication is needed. For example, it includes:

- Real-Time Chat Messaging (like Skype or Slack).
- One-Click Phone Calls (like Skype or Slack).
- Instant Video Conferencing (like GoToMeeting or Zoom).
- Screen Sharing (like GoToMeeting or Zoom).
- Real-Time 'Walkie-Talkie' Audio Messaging (like Zello or Voxer).

Here's a screenshot of what Team Chat looks like in Software Funnels:

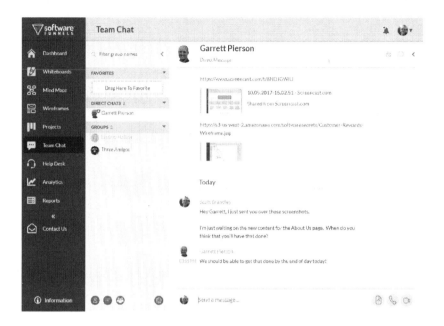

Having chat, phone, video, screen share and walkie-talkie at your fingertips gives you the ability to reach your team in a variety of different ways according to your particular needs. For example:

- The **chat tool** is ideal for quick messages throughout the day, but if you want to verbally express an idea, the **walkie-talkie** is awesome, and it gets added right into the messaging area so it becomes a natural part of the conversation.

- If you wanted to have a daily kickoff meeting with your pro-grammers, you could do a **video conference**, and actually see their faces and talk to them in person. You could even **share your screen**, or have them share theirs so you can see what they're working on right then.

- If you were looking at a project task in 'Projects' and had a question but didn't want to type it, you could call that particular person right from your computer in one click, using the **phone** option.

Regardless of whether you want to talk to one person, a small group, or your entire team, Team Chat gives you the ability to reach out however you see fit - all within one, easy to use communications tool.

Time Zones

As we've previously mentioned, a lot of our programmers are overseas. This makes it difficult to communicate sometimes, because there's only a small window where we're all working at the same time. We've made this work by asking our programmers to work a swing shift, which means that there are at least 3-4 hours of time each day when both teams are working. Because we typically pay them more than the average rate, they are willing to work around our schedule.

Just make sure that both parties are understanding of time zones and work times, as people have lives and families. Happy programmers make the process much more fun and efficient.

Daily Reports

Another important part of communication is feedback. One thing that we expect from members of our team, especially our programmers and designers, is that they send us a report at the end of every work day, using the 'Reports' tool in Software Funnels. This report summarizes what they accomplished that day, and contains any specific questions they may have. It also tells us if they ran into any issues that stopped their progression on a task.

Here is an example of one of our programmers' daily reports - (You can see a larger, color version if you go to www.SoftwareSecrets.com/report):

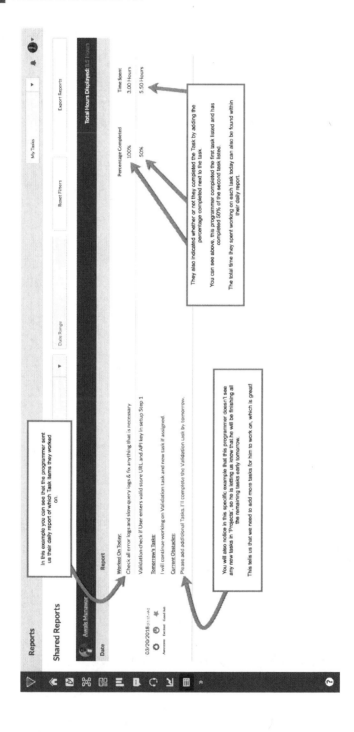

In this example you can see that the programmer sent us an update on the tasks he was assigned, and whether or not he completed them. On the task he didn't complete, he added 50% completed next to the task, which means they he estimated that he completed half the task.

You will also notice in this specific example that this programmer doesn't see any new tasks in 'Projects', so he is letting us know that he will be finishing the rest of the uncompleted tasks early tomorrow. This tells us that we need to add more tasks for him to work on, which is great!

These daily reports keep you in the loop, and make the programmer, designer, or any other team members you add, accountable for their work day. It also lets you know exactly what is getting done and what is left to do, so you can keep the ball rolling with task creation.

(If you aren't using Software Funnels, you can do reporting using email. Just request that your programmers email you a daily report, and make sure they include what they worked on and what percentage they have completed on each task.)

Screenshots and Videos

Another very important aspect of communication is how you deliver the tasks to your team. Each individual task has its own unique set of instructions, and you need to provide as much detail as you possibly can.

If you learn this one skill you will become a jedi master in project management.

This is where two more important tools come into play - screen capture (also known as screenshots) and screen recording (also known as screencasts). These two tools help give our programmers a visual example of what we are trying to explain. Honestly, if it weren't for these two tools, software development would make us want to pull our hair out! (Oh wait, we don't have any hair - nevermind.)

There are several free and paid screen capture and screen recording products out there. Here are just a few:

- **Snagit - Highly Recommended** - Everyone on our team uses Snagit because it does both screen capture and screen recording, and it's super easy to learn and use.
- Cloud App - getcloudapp.com (Much like Snagit, takes screenshots and screencasts)
- Fireshot (great free option for screenshots on PC's)
- Screencast-o-matic.com (creates screencast videos on PC's)
- CamStudio (creates screencast videos on PC's)
- Jing (a free lite version of Snagit with limited options)
- Screenflow (creates screencast videos on Macs)

We love Snagit because it does both screen capture and screencasting in the same tool. We would gladly pay $1,000 for Snagit if we had to, but fortunately it only costs $49 bucks. Another really nice feature is how fast it is to use. As soon as the screenshot or video is done, you simply click a button and it uploads to the web and saves a link right in your clipboard that you can paste and share – all within a few seconds.

Note: in our Software Secrets Training System we created a step-by-step training video on exactly how we use Snagit. To get access to the Software Secrets Training System, go to www.SoftwareSecrets.com/training.

The Devil is in the Details

Now that you have your team chat, your project management tool, your reporting tool, and your screen capture tools all in place ready to go, the last tool you're going to need is your brain. As you start adding tasks into 'Projects', you need to make sure that you're adding as much detail as you can to each task that you give your programmers.

When creating tasks for any members of your team, but especially for your programmers, the more detail you can provide, the better. This usually involves at least one or more screenshots, and, if a task is particularly challenging, at least one screencast.

But, before we move on, let's talk a bit more about screenshots. When you take a screenshot, you need to be very clear what you want the programmer to do with it. Always make sure that you are using arrows and text to clearly explain the details inside of your screenshots. It will go a long way to getting what you want done as fast as possible.

On your first few tasks, you also want to make sure that you chat with your programmers. Ask them to read over the task details and have them ask you any questions that they may have right then. We do this on a regular basis, especially when starting a new project or hiring a new programmer. It lets us know if we are on target with the amount of detail we're including in our tasks, based on each specific programmer's needs. It also allows us to know if the programmer understands the task. Over time you will get a feel as to how much detail you need to add to each task, and your programmer will get a feel for when they need to ask for clarification.

Here is an example of one of our detailed tasks that we added to 'Projects' in Software Funnels when we were building our software company, Customer Rewards. In order for you to easily read it, we copied the text from the actual task and pasted it below. (Note: All of the screencast.com URLs inside the task are active, so you can type them in any browser to see the level of information we're providing in our screenshots. You can also go to www.Software-Secrets.com/links for instant access to all of the screencast URLs.)

Task:

Create a new page for the admin dashboard area in Customer Rewards

Details:

We need to create a new page for the admin dashboard area here: http://www.screencast.com/t/sn6FjA4ZLRk

Name it "Create Billing Page".

On this page we need the following fields:
Page Name (if the page name already exists, then give warning to choose another name)
Setup Fee Price
Monthly Fee Price (Make Yearly) check box
"Create Billing Page" button

When user fills out fields ("Monthly Fee Price" is only required field), then it will create a billing page that is secure and forced https and looks like this:
https://www.screencast.com/t/Iih28ZmqkGid

http://www.screencast.com/t/yrsIGcfazo8
Salman should have this design, just get the design from him.

Here are the changes that need to be made for this new Customer Rewards version:

http://www.screencast.com/t/y1aaIC3OjDO

and

http://www.screencast.com/t/iAPA9MyuG

and

Next you can change all the fields here: http://www.screencast.com/t/dhXepOTRY to match what you need, e.g. from the create client page on admin dashboard: http://www.screencast.com/t/7NMi714kxp1

Anyone can have access to these pages.

They should be named like this: https://customerrewards.com/secure/{pagename}

This page should be hooked to Stripe API like the http://staging.customerrewards.com/admin/Clients/create page

so that when the visitor clicks "Checkout", it will charge the card.

Please add all necessary validation too.

Testing the Code

After each task is finished, you should expect your programmers to test the code they just created or updated, so make sure you communicate this by telling them that they should test everything before they move the task into the 'Completed - Ready to Test' column. Once they move the task into the 'Completed - Ready to Test' column, you also need to test it thoroughly as soon as possible. Keep in mind that programmers are not the best testers and that you are going to find bugs, errors and issues that need to be resolved. Try your best not to get mad or frustrated with them, as this is normal. The reason you need to test it right away is because that particular task is fresh in the programmer's mind, so the faster you can give them feedback, the better. Also, if the programmers know that you are always testing their code, over time, they will become more thorough, and you'll get more adept at providing better instructions.

Bottom line, if you test thoroughly now, it will mitigate the problems and bugs down the line.

Get Some Rest

You might be surprised to find a section about resting in this chapter, but when managing a project it can become very tempting to work late hours, especially if your programmers and designers are overseas. Remember that in order to be effective, both you and your programming team need rest.

Fresh eyes are always important, and the mind often solves problems while you sleep. Also keep in mind that a tired programmer is an ineffective programmer, so don't force your programmers to keep your schedule. It's much better to allow them to work during a swing shift and overlap part of your day, than to force them to work a night shift in order to be available during your entire work day. If you set it up right, as we mentioned earlier in the chapter, you can usually find a window where you're both available and alert.

The same advice applies to you. <u>Don't stay up till all hours of the morning in an effort to be available for your programmers</u>. It's not worth it. Not only does it rob you of sleep, but it causes your programmers to create an unhealthy dependency on you. It's much better to give them detailed tasks, and then discuss things early in the morning during that window when you're both available.

Give Them Praise

It is so important that as the leader you tell your team how amazing they are doing on a continual basis. A simple and sincere, "You're doing a great job!" will do. Make sure to celebrate the little wins as well as the big wins.

As the project progresses, take time to find out more about your team. Are they married? Do they have a family? If so, how many children do they have? What are their hobbies? This will show them that you care, and it will make them more loyal and engaged.

Final Thoughts - Important!

Now that you've officially started programming your software and development is underway, you need to make sure that the project continues to move at a proper pace. Ultimately, the progress and success of your company are up to you, but as the business owner and most likely the project manager at this stage, you must be completely aware of what's going on, and always be two steps ahead, otherwise the project will slow down, or even come to a grinding halt. Every single day you need to evaluate where you are in the development process and where you are going.

To help you stay on track, we've added some thoughts below that we feel are important to bring up or re-emphasize. These are in no particular order, but they're all important for your success:

- **Remember that you are the boss.** You're in charge of making sure that everyone gets their work done, and people are going to depend on you for direction and guidance. You may not always know the answer to everything and that's okay, just do the best you can. If you get stumped, or hit a roadblock, that's the perfect time to go on a walk and get some fresh air. We are convinced that going on walks has been one of the keys to our success.

- **Communicate, communicate, communicate.** Always remember that project management lives or dies based on the level of communication between the project manager and the team. As the project manager, 'Projects' and 'Team Chat' are your lifelines. You must keep your programmer's tasks constantly up to date and prioritized so you know which tasks are moving along and when you need to give them more tasks.

■ **Test, test, test.** Each day you need to be testing items that the team has completed. Testing throughout the entire programming process will make the beta testing process less painful, (we discuss beta testing in the next chapter). As you test the functionality and code, make sure that you share your findings with the programming team, (i.e. any updates, changes, errors, bugs, etc).

■ **Separate critical and non-critical tasks.** Whenever you come up with new tasks, add these tasks to your own hidden 'Projects' board to release later. It's a good idea to create two separate columns; one named 'Critical Tasks' and one named 'Non-Critical Tasks', and then to sort both your critical and non-critical tasks from highest to lowest priority. This makes it easy to move tasks to the programmers when they complete one or more of their 3 tasks. Always move tasks from the Critical column first. Then, once all of your critical tasks are completed or moved to the 'Completed - Ready to Test' column on the programmer's board, then start moving non-critical tasks over.

■ **Try to avoid 'scope creep'.** Scope creep is when a project grows beyond its anticipated size because you start adding more features than you had originally planned. This can be a slippery slope, and you are bound to run into it, so you need to be aware of it. As new features or ideas pop up, you will start to think, "Oh, that would be awesome", or "I think our customers would love it if our software could do this". Scope creep or feature bloat can significantly delay your launch, and cause you to spend a lot more money and time on development.

It is important that you stick to your original version 1.0 plan as closely as possible. Always have your Minimum Viable Product (MVP) in mind. There can always be a version 2, 3 and beyond, but you need to stay focused and get your MVP to market, even though it's not perfect.

We are not saying that things can't change during development. Odds are that the wireframe mockups that you initially created probably had one or two missing elements, and the layout or functionality that you envisioned will probably need to be adjusted to a degree. This is perfectly fine. Just be careful that the entire project doesn't change from the original concept, or your progress will be completely derailed.

- **Ask your programmers for their opinion.** Let them know that it's okay for them to share their thoughts or give you feedback. Your way may not always be the right way to do something, so give your programmers the ability to share their expertise and experience when it counts.

We always let our programmers have a voice, and if they think something can be done better or differently, we give them the freedom to try it. We just make sure that they communicate the change of plan to us, and we let them know that we still make the final decision. If they present an idea that you don't like or that takes you away from the tasks at hand, just be honest and tell them how you feel. As long as you tell them in a respectful way, they will honor your decision.

If the programmer does come up with a better idea or a more effective way to go about doing something, thank them and give them kudos. If it's a big idea that saves you a significant amount of time or money, send them a gift or a bonus with their next check. It will mean a lot to them, and will encourage them to work harder and to keep looking for innovative solutions.

Project Management as a Life Skill

Hopefully, at this point in the book, your head is spinning (in a good way) from all of the incredibly valuable information we've given you. But, if for some reason you've got nothing from reading this book other than how to effectively manage a project, then what you've learned is worth its weight in gold!

Effective project management is a highly valuable, highly sought after skill that is a HUGE differentiator in the workplace. What we've shared with you in this chapter, when properly learned and executed, will give you an invaluable skill set that will benefit the rest of your life.

In our Software Secrets Training System, we have a special bonus section called 'Project Management Secrets', where we personally share with you everything we know about how to effectively manage projects and teams. The great thing about this training is that we use our actual software companies as examples, so you can see real world project management in action.

Honestly, project management is one of the software secrets that has helped us to create multi-million dollar companies. It's one of the key differentiators between turning your idea into an Inc. 500 company, or just having a dream that you try to make a reality but never really takes off.

If you want to learn more about effective project management, we highly recommend that you go to www.SoftwareSecrets.com/training, and watch our introductory video.

CHAPTER 6

Beta Testing

The Beta Test - Your Stepping Stone to Success

Once you've put the necessary time and effort in, and version 1.0 (your MVP) of your software is finished, you are ready to start the beta testing process.

Running an effective beta test can give you the opportunity to collect valuable feedback and information, like: What errors or bugs keep coming up? Are any key features missing? Are beta testers happy with the product? Is your product ready to be launched to the public?

A huge benefit of a beta test is that you have the opportunity to collect case studies and testimonials for your marketing material. A beta test also allows you to gather feedback and data that can help with future features and improvements to the product. You can also use the beta test as a launching tool to get people that didn't make it into your beta test, interested in your actual launch.

In the last chapter we mentioned the importance of you and your team testing your software's code and functionality. If you tested your code throughout the programming process, you will be much more prepared for the beta testing process.

During the beta test, things may go really well, and your testers will give you accolades and praise your new software, or it may go really bad and your testers end up not liking it or actively using it. If things take a turn for the worst, you are going to need very thick skin to weather the storm. With a beta test comes potential criticism and possible issues you never could have anticipated. Negative feedback can be particularly hard to handle, especially after all the time and effort you've put in, but the way you use this feedback can determine the ultimate failure or success of your software.

The best approach to take when going into the beta test phase is to acknowledge and accept that your software isn't perfect. Even if you thought you covered everything, the reality is that you haven't. This is just part of the process, so don't take it personally. The key is to be willing to fight through it, and continue improving your product until it becomes what the consumer wants or needs.

In order to pull off a successful beta test, you need a plan. The following are items you need to consider when planning out your beta test:

- How long will the beta test run?
- How many beta testers do you need?
- How are you going to recruit beta testers?
- How will beta testers communicate with you?
- Are you going to make them sign any agreements?
- Are you going to do an exit survey at the end of the test?

We've expounded on these questions below to help give you some direction when putting together and launching your beta test:

How Long Will the Beta Test Run?

When we do a beta test, our goal is to run it for a minimum of six weeks, but no longer than 12 weeks. We feel that this gives our testers a decent amount of time to use the software, but it also allows us get it to market as soon as possible. You need to set a goal date for the beta test to end. It's important to write this date down and make sure everyone on your team knows it. Also, make sure that your beta testers know this date so that expectations are set.

The amount of time that you run your beta test really depends on what you are trying to achieve. If you are trying to simply find bugs, then this test can run pretty quick. If you are trying to collect data or create case studies, then the beta test may take longer.

As we mentioned before, the product will never be perfect – you just want your MVP to be launch-ready.

How many Beta Testers do you need?

We usually try and get at least 10 beta testers on the low end, and no more than 30 on the high end. Ultimately, the number of beta testers you need really depends on what you feel is needed based on the software you've created and your target market. The main reason to keep it in this range is that it helps to keep things more manageable.

How are you going to Recruit Beta Testers?

There are several ways you can find and recruit beta testers to join your beta test. Here are a few options:

- **Offer incentives to people you know.** In many cases, offering an incentive to people in your own circle of influence can go a long way in getting people interested in testing your software. Some examples of incentives are; gift cards, free temporary access to your new software, a special discount on your service, or personalized gifts. You can even offer people a prestigious title, like 'founding member' instead of beta tester, and play to their ego.

- **Hire beta testers.** There are some resources online where you can actually hire people to help you to announce your beta test or who will help you find beta testers. Some of these resources are free and some are paid, but as with most things in life, you get what you pay for. Here are a few options:
  - Betabound.com/announce/
  - Betafy.co
  - Betafamily.com
  - Usertesting.com

- **Recruit on relevant forums and social sites.** If your software is relevant to a specific target market, and you can find forums where these people tend to hang out, then this is a great place to look for recruits during your beta test initially, and also to market to later once you're ready to launch.

- **Advertise on Google or Facebook.** Another way to get in front of your target market is to run ads using Google Adwords or Facebook Ads to get your beta test in front of your potential target market. Then, once you have enough recruits, simply turn off your ad campaign.

- **Reach out to your Opt-in list.** If you followed our 12 Steps in Chapter 4, then you should have created an opt-in page as the landing page of your website during your development phase. There's a really good chance that anyone who opted in is very interested in being a beta tester. Simply send them an email and ask them if they would be interested in joining your beta test.

How Will Beta Testers Communicate With You?

You are going to need a way for your beta testers to communicate with you, in order to send you any feedback or bug reports.

Typically, we've used our own Rhino Support software, where we'll add a 'Live Chat' and "Enter Feedback" widget on all the control panel / backend pages of the site we're beta testing, but if you're a Software Funnels member, you can use the 'Help Desk' tool for this.

As far as actual communication, you need to be very clear with each beta tester as to what information you are looking to get from them, such as bugs, feature requests, flow or user interface issues, etc. You need to get them to say that they will send you feedback, or even better, have them apply to be in the beta testing program and make it a requirement to send feedback. It also helps for you to communicate frequently with your test group as a whole, keeping them up to date on the project so they feel like they're included in the process.

Once you start collecting feedback from your test group, remember that you don't have to make every change or suggestion that your testers recommend. It is very likely that several of their suggestions will make a lot of sense and would even be great features or tools, but more often than not they will also add significant development time to your project. While it's important to fix any glitches or bugs in your software, and add any crucial functionality that you may have missed, the Minimum Viable Product (MVP) is still the overall goal at this point, so make sure to keep that in mind.

You will find that some beta testers will compare your product to other similar products on the market. They will probably suggest features or functionality that work like what they are used to, or what they have seen before. In these cases, thank them for their feedback, and tell them that you will consider their suggestions in future versions of the software. Even if their feedback is overly critical and negative, try your best to stay positive, and don't lose sight of the bigger picture, and your overall goals.

The ultimate goal of your beta test should be to try to find and resolve as many critical issues and bugs as possible, while trying your best to only add features and tools that are absolutely necessary to launch an effective MVP. Just remember that if you do add any features, it will take double the time you expect to implement them.

Are you going to make them sign any agreements?

When signing up beta test users, we recommend that you create a beta test agreement and a non-disclosure agreement (NDA). This just helps to protect your intellectual property before your software is officially launched to the public.

Here is a beta test agreement that works great:
https://www.upcounsel.com/beta-test-agreement

And here is an NDA agreement:
http://www.ndasforfree.com/NDAS/GetSoftwareBeta.html

We are not lawyers by any means, so please seek appropriate legal counsel before using these resources.

Are you going to do an exit survey at the end of the test?

Once you are ready to end the beta program, you should have all the participants complete a short exit survey. If there is an incentive or a contest, make it a requirement to complete the survey in order to qualify.

It is essential that you ask your beta testers specific questions that will help you to understand how the beta test went for them and how they liked the product.

Here are some questions that we feel should be required:

- Name and email
- How much did you use the product? (multiple choice with amount of hours)

- What was your overall impression (scale of 1-10)
- How would you rate different key features (scale of 1-10, and then break out the features for them to rate individually)
- Do you feel like the product is ready to sell to the public? (yes or no, and why)
- What do you feel could be improved? (paragraph field)
- Would you recommend this product to a friend? (scale of 1-10)

Some of the survey tools that you can use for this survey are Google Forms, Wufoo.com, and Surveymonkey.com.

Once someone completes the survey, you can use their feedback to determine if they would be an ideal contact for a testimonial. If a beta tester had a good experience, there is a very good chance that they will not only give you a good review, but give you an actual testimonial that you can leverage on your website and use as social proof during your marketing campaign. If they are willing to give you a testimonial, ask them for a picture or even a video so you can use it as part of their testimonial - it will add more credibility.

Taking The Next Step...

At this point, we have taught you virtually everything you need to know to build any type of software product that you can imagine. In addition, we've done our best to share with you every software secret, strategy, tip and trick that we've learned throughout our entire careers that have enabled Shopper Approved to make the Inc. 500 not once, but twice, and to build our own thriving software empire.

We hope that what you've read so far has inspired you as to what's possible, and what you can do with a little bit of focus and determination.

Now that you know how to build the software, it's time to focus on the front end marketing. This is where our long-time friend and business partner, Russell Brunson, comes into play. Russell is a big reason why this book exists, because ultimately, what he created allows you to market and sell your new software product faster, easier and more successfully than ever before.

As we mentioned in the beginning of the book, just like us, Russell built his online, multi-million dollar empire selling software. But, as luck would have it, rather than focusing on developing software like we did, he focused instead on the marketing side, and he became one of the most revered online marketing experts in the world. In fact, he consults for people like Tony Robbins, Marcus Lemonis, and Robert Kiyosaki.

As you can imagine, this created an interesting dynamic in our relationship over the years. We (Scott and Garrett) ultimately became software experts, and Russell became an online marketing expert. We always knew that someday, if we could just come up with the right timing and circumstances, together we would do something epic.

Then in 2014, Russell launched ClickFunnels.

You probably don't realize it right now, but ClickFunnels is the vessel that will make your software empire a reality. In all of our years online, there has never been a marketing tool that can make more people wealthy faster than ClickFunnels can.

We know that's hard to comprehend at this point, so let us try to express it in another way.

There is a hallway in Russell's office in Boise, Idaho, that is over 30 feet long and at least 10 feet high that is literally covered in picture frames of golden records on both sides from top to bottom. If you didn't know better, you would think that you were in a record studio looking at albums that had gone double platinum. But these records have nothing to do with music. Each one of these records represents a front end sales funnel that was built using ClickFunnels that has made over one million dollars in sales. There are currently over 250 of them, and ClickFunnels is only four years old.

Do we have your attention now?

When you combine the power of Software Secrets and Software Funnels (on the backend) with the power of ClickFunnels (on the front end), pure magic happens, and the possibilities become incredibly exciting! In fact, we built Software Funnels so that it integrates seamlessly with ClickFunnels.

Now, keep in mind that you don't actually have to start using Click-Funnels until you've finished developing your software, but we feel that it's very important for you to know how It works and how it will ultimately help you to quickly build and grow your software empire when you're ready.

The next chapter gives you an enlightening overview of ClickFunnels, why it's so important to your success, and how it can help you to literally skyrocket your sales!

CHAPTER 7

Sales Funnels

How Junk Mail Can Make You Rich

As we mentioned in the last chapter, like us, Russell Brunson generates millions of dollars in recurring revenue selling software, but his superpower is actually in online marketing.

In fact, we would say that Russell and his team have cracked the code on how to sell pretty much anything online, including physical products, info products, and of course, software products. He did this by immersing himself in sales ever since he was a teenager. He used to sign up for every free report and piece of junk mail he could get his hands on, and then when he would get home from school, he would study them and break them down, just so he could understand how they tried to market and sell their products and services.

What he found is that most companies would offer a free or low-cost product or service up front, and then make money through additional upsells and promotions. This is called a sales funnel. If you picture a funnel, it's wide at the top and then narrows down.

The way a sales funnel works is that you sell your free or low-cost offer first to get the most people in your target market as possible into the top of funnel, then you progressively upsell your customers more valuable products or services, and you keep doing this until you reach the bottom of the funnel, where you sell your most expensive, most valuable product or service to a small, elite percentage of your customers who can afford it. As customers progress through the sales funnel they naturally drop off according to their needs and financial ability to continue.

These sales funnels are what allowed companies that were marketing using direct mail to be successful offline for decades before the internet really took off.

The defining moment for Russell was when he realized that the exact same sales techniques that people were using in the offline world could also work in the online world. Once he realized this, he went to work adapting the puzzle pieces to work online. Instead of direct mail, he used email. Instead of networking, he used Facebook. Instead of TV, he used YouTube. Instead of radio, he used podcasts. Instead of newspaper ads, he used PPC ads and blogs.

Over the years, Russell would focus on very particular areas of online marketing, and build info products and software tools around each of them. He created dozens of products and software tools that helped people find traffic, collect emails, optimize PPC ads, create webinars and podcasts, build blogs, write killer sales scripts and content, generate landing and squeeze pages, and the list goes on.

He even ran over 1,000 different split tests over the years to find out what strategies got the best results over time.

All of this work and effort took Russell the better part of a decade, and at the end of it, he had helped tens of thousands of people, but all of his software tools worked independently of each other, which made it incredibly difficult for his customers to successfully leverage them in their businesses.

This is how ClickFunnels was born.

ClickFunnels 101

Ultimately, Russell took all of his software tools, re-engineered them, improved them, and put them all together into one incredible solution that not only creates any type of sales funnel, but also creates stunningly beautiful websites and web pages that are optimized for maximum conversion.

With ClickFunnels, you can instantly create landing pages, squeeze pages, video pages, email opt-in pages, upsell pages, downsell pages, webinar pages, checkout pages, one-time offer pages, and pretty much any other type of page you can imagine.

You can also create membership sites, webinars and entire webinar email sequences, split tests, affiliate and partner accounts, and you can directly tie into multiple payment gateways, including Stripe for recurring billing.

For anyone wanting to develop a software product to sell online (that means you), ClickFunnels is truly a dream come true!

Now, keep in mind that you don't have to use ClickFunnels. You could always go get your own hosting account, build your own website and landing pages, set up your own email services, create your own autoresponders, build out and manage your own sales funnels and tracking system, integrate your own opt-in forms, set up your own affiliate program, develop your own checkout pages, and then get all of these products to play nicely together.

Or, you could just ask someone to hand you a hammer so you can repeatedly hit yourself in the head with it!

Before ClickFunnels, we used to do all of this manually, because there was no other real way to do it. In fact, we still do this on some of our bigger sites, and it costs us tens of thousands of dollars a year just to continue to improve and maintain them.

With ClickFunnels, every tool you need is already integrated, ready for you to use at the click of a button. That is amazing in itself, but the best part is that it creates absolutely beautiful pages that flow seamlessly between one another. One thing that we've learned over the years is that 'perception is reality', which means that whatever people see they will tend to believe. So, if someone comes to your website and it looks likes a million bucks, then it immediately has credibility, which means that more people will be willing to trust you and buy from you.

ClickFunnel pages always look like a million bucks and have been split tested for optimal results.

The other really cool thing about ClickFunnels, is that there are dozens of sales funnel templates already created that you can just run with. This way you don't have to reinvent the wheel. But, if you really want a super custom website and sales funnel, there is an entire marketplace full of ClickFunnel certified experts that you can hire to help you.

ClickFunnels is truly a force of nature that is literally changing the way that sales are made on the internet. There is no other product like it in the world. In fact, since you're reading this book right now, there's a very good chance that you've already seen ClickFunnels in action.

Software Secrets uses ClickFunnels.

Not only is our landing page built with it, but our sales funnel, and our entire Software Secrets Training System is also built using it. In addition, we run our webinars through it and handle all of our sales transactions (including recurring billing), and our affiliates and partnerships through it.

It is an absolute lifesaver, and if you use any other option than ClickFunnels to build out and manage your front end sales funnels, then you are really doing yourself a huge disservice.

DotCom Secrets and Expert Secrets

At the end of the day, ClickFunnels is an amazing tool.

But that's all it is - it's just a tool. Just like Software Funnels is a tool. Just like a shovel is a tool. Or a wrench.

The reality is that for any tool to have any real value, you have to learn how to effectively use it.

To help you learn how to effectively use ClickFunnels, Russell has written two amazing books. One is called 'DotCom Secrets', and the other is called 'Expert Secrets'.

DotCom Secrets teaches you everything you need to know or ever wanted to know about sales funnels, and marketing and growing your company online. In this book, Russell teaches you about:

- Value ladders and sales funnels
- How to find your dream customers
- The 3 types of traffic
- How to create an attractive character
- How to create engaging email sequences
- The 23 building blocks of a successful sales funnel
- The top 7 most popular sales funnels

He also gives you proven templates and scripts that you can use in your marketing efforts. Bottom line, DotCom Secrets is a wealth of information that can ignite your entire sales process, and maximize your software sales.

After Russell wrote DotCom Secrets, he then went on to write Expert Secrets, which teaches anyone how to become an expert, and create a passionate tribe of followers and paying customers. The information in this book is very important because it teaches you how to position yourself as an expert in your market, and more importantly, to your potential customers. In Expert Secrets, you learn things like:

- How to create a mass movement
- How to become a charismatic leader
- How to effectively use persuasion to sell

- How to start a cause that people can get behind
- How to design an opportunity 'switch' (this is brilliant)
- How to create belief patterns
- How to build a stackable offer

Honestly, in our opinion, these two books are more valuable in terms of immediate actionable sales results than any other books we've ever read. They are incredibly well written, and have tons of images and drawings to help you to visually connect with the key points and principles that Russell is trying to teach you.

Don't Get Distracted!

We know that this is going to sound absolutely ridiculous after we've spent this entire chapter singing the praises of ClickFunnels and Russell's books; DotCom Secrets and Expert Secrets, and we know that they sound very interesting and intriguing, but please, if you haven't already read them, do not read them yet.

If you already signed up for ClickFunnels in Chapter 4, so you could complete Step 12 and create your opt-in page, then that's fine, but once your opt-in page is up, leave ClickFunnels alone until your software is nearing completion.

If you do anything else, it will just become a distraction at this point.

You have to stay focused on building out your software product first, otherwise you'll have nothing to sell and no reason to actually create your sales funnel.

Once your software is in beta testing, that's a great time to really start focusing on your front end design and your sales funnel. At that point, we suggest that you dive head first into both DotCom Secrets and Expert Secrets, and then use what you learn to make your website and sales funnel rock!

Software Funnels and ClickFunnels

At the end of the day, the only two pieces of software that you need to launch a successful software company are Software Funnels and ClickFunnels.

Software Funnels gives you the ability to effectively build and manage your entire backend software development process, and ClickFunnels gives you the ability to easily and effectively build and manage your entire front end website and sales funnel, including your checkout and recurring billing.

These two software tools work seamlessly together to create the optimal environment for you to succeed in building your own software empire.

CHAPTER 8

It's Time to Launch!

Congratulations!

You came up with an amazing software idea and turned it into a real, bonafide product. That is a major accomplishment, and you should be very proud of what you've done. Now that you're done beta testing your product, and your front end sales funnel is in place, the real fun begins – it's finally time to share your baby with the world! This is going to take some serious effort on your part, but if you do it correctly, it will pay you back dividends for the rest of your life.

Many people erroneously believe that an amazing product is all that's needed to attract customers and build a business. They have an 'if you build it, they will come' mentality. Unfortunately, it doesn't matter how good your product is if no one knows about it. And, even if people do know about it, your software must be marketed to the right target market in the right way for it to be successful.

Here are some important tips and strategies that will help you to successfully launch your software business:

- Launch now, fix later
- Sales vs marketing

- Generate leads
- Look for strategic partners
- Know your numbers
- Continue improving your product

We discuss each of these in more detail below...

Launch Now, Fix Later

Unless serious issues and bugs were found in your beta test that stop you from hitting the gas, right now is the best time to launch. The hardest thing when starting out is trying to make decisions with little or no real-world data. Making your software live forces you to play in the real world with real consequences, in order to get the data and feedback you need to make those important decisions.

You may be scared and a little hesitant, which is normal, but don't let it stop you from launching. The longer you postpone your launch, the longer you postpone your potential for recurring revenue and growth. The only way any software company ever made it was by launching a flawed product.

Another important reason why you need to launch now is that you can start getting real customers, so you can leverage their experiences and social proof. That way you can 'prove' to other potential clients that your software is viable, valuable, and worth their time and monetary investment.

It's time to put your guerrilla marketing hat on and really start thinking about how to make connections with influencers in your target market. If you happen to know anyone with any kind of influence in your space, now's the time to ask them for a favor. If you don't know anyone, now's the time to start making new friends.

As part of your launch, come up with a list of your top ten dream clients or influencers, and think of some fun, creative ways to reach out to them and offer your software services for free in exchange for a review and/or a case study. If none of them bite, then make another list and keep going until some of them take you up on your offer. This is going to go a long way in getting you amazing feedback, real data, and important case studies and testimonials that you and your sales team can use to establish credibility and build your brand.

When Scott and his father launched one of their very first software products, they were part of a group of online business owners who met weekly through regular emails and conference calls. Their software product came out of a need that all these people expressed on the call and in their emails. Once they created a product that solved the problem, they naturally went to that group and offered them free access in exchange for feedback. Not only did they get great feedback from the group, but their innovative efforts got the attention of a major online influencer, who then personally invited them to a private mastermind event in Las Vegas, which then led to a partnership on their next software product, which created an instant revenue stream of $20,000/mo that lasted for nearly 2 years.

Bottom line, launch your product (even if you don't feel ready), and get to know people in your industry. You'll be amazed at how fast doors can open for you.

Sales vs Marketing

Your entire life, you've probably heard the term sales and marketing thousands of times, thinking that they were basically the same thing. In reality they are very different, and it's important that you understand why, and how they work together, if you want to run a successful software company.

Marketing is all about sharing your brand and your brand message, and how you communicate and position that message. The goal of marketing is to reach, attract, educate and engage your target market through various means of interaction, which are typically accomplished through your website, articles, paid advertising, videos, press releases, social media, blogs, etc. Think of marketing as the precursor to sales. You can't sell anything until you market what you're selling.

Sales, on the other hand, is the process of taking a prospect that has consumed your marketing message in one or more forms, and then persuading them to make a purchase. Sales can be done with or without human interaction, but the more compelling your marketing message is, and the more targeted your market is, the more sales you will make.

The reason it's important to understand the difference is because you will need to learn and utilize both skills at different times. There will be times where you will need to put on your marketing hat to attract potential buyers, and then there will be times when you will need to put on your sales hat to close the deal. Knowing the difference helps you to set up correct strategies for maximum results.

Another way to look at it, is that marketing is like dating. You first want to get to know someone and go on some dates to make sure you're compatible. Then, when the time is right, you get married, or make the sale. Also, keep in mind that you should never try and close a sale just for the money if you know someone is not a good fit for your product. Just like a bad marriage, it might be fun during the honeymoon phase, but you will probably regret it and end up paying for it in the long run.

Generate Leads

Part of your marketing effort involves gathering leads of prospects that you can sell to.

There are many ways in which you can attract and gather leads for your sales process. These lead sources are called channels, and they include:

- Websites
- Sales Funnels/opt-in pages (e.g. ClickFunnels)
- Webinars (check out Russell's perfectwebinarsecrets.com)
- Email marketing
- Advertising (e.g. Facebook, Google, Twitter Ads)
- Social media
- Lead databases/lists for sale
- Blogging/guest blogging
- Content marketing
- Video marketing (e.g. YouTube, Facebook Live)
- Affiliate marketing
- Joint ventures
- Podcasting
- Cold calling
- Door to door
- Events (e.g. trade shows, expos)
- Speaking engagements
- Magazines
- Teleseminars
- Direct mail

One of the keys to gathering leads is determining who your target market is and where they hang out. The key is to go to those places where your market congregates, and then figure out how to communicate with them and share your marketing message.

As you consider which lead channels to use, here are some questions to ask yourself:

- What channels are best suited to my target market (best fit)?
- What do I think is the best channel to focus on first, second, third?
- How much am I willing to spend in order to gain one customer with this channel?
- How many total customers do I think I can get with this channel?
- Which channel can give me the most low-hanging fruit?

Focus on the channel that seems the most promising, and go from there. We suggest that you never focus on more than two or three channels at a time, otherwise you will quickly become overwhelmed and inefficient. Once you have built processes and know that you are doing a good job with your top three channels, and have created proven systems that allow those channels to run without your direct intervention, then you can add more channels.

When gathering leads, the most important information is the prospect's name, email address and/or phone number. Email marketing is one of the best and most efficient ways to move a prospect through your sales process. If you can get a phone number, that's even better, as you then have a way to have a one-on-one personal conversation with that lead, and the sales process can move forward a lot faster.

If you are in a business-to-business (B2B) market, then you will more than likely be able to purchase leads. This is how we have grown our businesses over the past several years. Since we know our target market is ecommerce companies, we find businesses that sell ecommerce company lists, take that data, add it into Hubspot, the Customer Relationship Management (CRM) software that we use to manage our sales leads, and have our sales agents reach out directly to those leads via phone and email. This is how

Shopper Approved became an Inc. 500 company and one of the fastest growing software companies in America.

Here are some list companies you can start with: Infousa.com, Social123.com, Datanyze.com, and PipeCandy.com. You are going to want to research the best options for your specific target market to find the best fit for you.

Purchasing leads is not the end all, but it can be a great catalyst to helping you and your sales team to start turning leads into prospects, and then into sales.

Look for Strategic Partners

Getting joint venture partners and affiliates to help you sell your product should be a big part of your strategy. It takes some time and effort to get things up and running, but it can pay off big.

The key is to get one big player to partner with you, and then use that partner's name as leverage to get more big partners.

Russell has had incredible success with strategic partnerships, and has put together a great video about how to find your dream partners. He calls it 'Finding your Dream 100'. Learn about the Dream 100 here: www.SoftwareSecrets.com/dream-100

Know Your Numbers

By far, the best analogy we can give you to teach you the importance of knowing your numbers is the analogy of the water bucket.

Sales is the water pouring into the bucket. The more sales you make, the more water fills the bucket.

Churn is the number of holes in the bucket. Every customer that cancels leaves a hole where water leaves the bucket.

Your job is to know how much water is coming into the bucket, and how many holes there are in the bucket at any given time.

In a SAAS business, sales are entirely pointless if you can't keep your customers actively paying you over time. Peter Drucker once said the purpose of a business is to make and keep a customer. The term "churn" is the number of paying clients you lose over time, therefore, to lower churn, you need to focus on customer retention (we referred to customer retention as 'stickiness' in Chapter 2).

Focusing on customer retention should be just as important as marketing and sales.

Although we've mentioned churn multiple times in the book, this was a principle that we didn't always understand the importance of. For several years we would pride ourselves on making new sales, but we completely missed the boat on customer retention. We were basically pouring in water (sales), but were oblivious to the holes (churn), and wondering why our shoes were all wet!

The first step in understanding customer retention is to track it. Using services like baremetrics.com, chartmogul.com or 'Analytics' in Software Funnels, can quickly provide you with your customer churn, month to month and year to year, so you can know how well you are doing over time.

Once you know where you are, you should set some goals on improving it.

The easiest way to improve your customer retention is to have first-class customer support. One thing that we have implemented in some of our businesses is setting up a dedicated account manager for each client. This may not work for your business, but it has been an amazing customer retention tool for us.

Another thing we've implemented is paying our support team bonuses based on hitting low monthly churn rates. This motivates them to try and save customer's who are trying to cancel or whose credit card has expired or declined, and it's significantly lowered our churn.

Here are other some things you can do to improve your customer retention rate:

- **Set customer expectations up front, so they know how to best** use and utilize your software solution
- Onboard fast and efficiently so you don't lose their attention, excitement or momentum
- Get them results as fast as possible, so they see the value of your product
- Create customer education content to train them on your product
- Be proactive, not reactive
- Make your support personal
- Reinforce your product's value often
- Continually improve your product over time, and let them know about it
- Make communication between you and your customer as easy and effortless as possible
- Survey your clients regularly
- Lower pricing for clients when necessary
- Get clients to pay yearly instead of monthly (we always give clients 12 months for the price of 10 if they pay yearly - it works really well)
- Use contracts (Many companies do this to lower churn, but contracts don't work for every market. We highly recommend that you only do contracts if the customer wants long-term discount pricing or some kind of a deal.)
- WOW your customers by exceeding expectations

Your customer support team is your first line of defense against churn, so make sure that they are aware of it, and that they understand how it affects the company's overall revenues and success.

Continue Improving Your Product

Throughout this book we've focused on the fact that you need to build out your Minimum Viable Product (MVP). Now that you've completed version 1.0, and have launched it, you have the opportunity to start envisioning what version 2.0 will look like. Product innovation and improvement are extremely important for you to stay relevant and to add more value over time.

Improvement and innovation can and should be a part of every aspect of your software business, including your product, customer support, onboarding, marketing, sales, processes, employees, teams, culture, etc.

You need to be constantly improving and innovating to stay ahead of the competition and to help with customer retention. People are more distracted today than ever before, and you must keep their attention, even if they are already a paying client. This can be accomplished by continuing to create new features that benefit the customer over time. To achieve that, you need out-of-the-box thinking and innovation, rather than feature bloat.

The way you innovate and improve is by being aware of where you are. Take a step back and evaluate daily, or at least weekly, as to where you are currently, then consider where you want to be or think you should be, create a plan and goals to help you get there, and then go do what's necessary.

It's also important that you follow what is going on in your industry. Keep up to date by reading trade magazines and blogs, going to events/trade shows, and following experts or thought leaders. Also, make sure that you know what the competition is doing. You can easily do this by setting up Google Alerts at Google.com/alerts. This free service allows you to enter keywords (in this case, your competitor's names) and it sends you any information about that keyword daily, weekly, or as it happens. It's also a good idea to add alerts for your own company name to see what content is being created about you.

CHAPTER 9

Mistakes We Wish We Had Avoided

To end our book, we thought that it would be fun to share with you some of the mistakes, myths and preconceptions that have slowed down our progress at different times in our software careers. We hope that sharing these will help you to avoid some of the pain, problems and issues on your own journey.

No matter how hard you try to avoid them, you are bound to run into unforeseen issues and roadblocks along your path. This is just part of the process of building a business. If you accept that now and understand that all businesses go through it, it will help you get through those difficult times.

The items below are not in any particular order of significance, but they all played a role in our pain, struggles, and eventual breakthroughs and victories. We had to go through them all in order to get to where we are today. We don't consider any of them failures, but rather, we consider them learning experiences that ultimately helped us to be more successful.

Perfection will never be a reality

All of us want to be amazing at what we do. We want people to think that what we create is perfect and awesome. Our egos play a big role in how we deal with people and our decisions, but when it comes to software, you have to accept that it will never be anywhere even close to perfect. The reality is that if your software is mostly functional on a good day, then you're winning!

Don't let your pursuit for perfection cripple your success. The most successful companies launch their products when they are far from perfect, and then they improve them over time.

Take Facebook for example.

Facebook in 2004 (left) compared to Facebook in 2018 (right)

When Facebook first started out, it was a super low-budget rating site made from Harvard 'facebook' profiles that Mark Zuckerberg hacked, which rated how hot the girls at his alma mater were. But as the service grew and improved over time, it got better and better. It is now a fine-tuned behemoth that connects billions of people around the world, and is worth billions of dollars.

Instead of perfection, your goal should be getting something launched, even if it sucks at first, and then improving it over time.

Expect something totally different

If we've learned anything about software, it's that change is the only thing that remains constant. The reality is that the vision you have for your software today, will ultimately end up totally different than you could ever imagine. Every single one of our successful software products is completely different than what we thought it would be when we originally came up with it. If you can accept the idea that change allows innovation and improvement, it will be much easier for you to embrace it.

Pivot quickly

When changes do come, you must be able and willing to pivot quickly to adapt. If you don't make the hard and important decisions that are often forced by change, you and your company will be left behind in the dust. Software companies that can change and innovate quickly are the ones that grow and last.

With all our software businesses, we've had to pivot quickly at certain times and make hard decisions.

Sometimes this meant removing someone from the team. Other times it meant taking the company in a new direction due to changes in the industry we were in, or even shutting down or selling companies in order to pursue bigger opportunities.

Most of the pivots we've made were hard at first, but ended up being positive. For example:

- Doubling, tripling, and even quadrupling our prices in order to stay in line with our competition gave us the opportunity to drastically increase our revenue and make even more sales, when we initially thought that our sales would go way down.

- Hiring more team members gave us the opportunity to focus on scaling the business, which helped us grow a lot faster, even though it was difficult financially at the time.

- Starting a call center and limiting our online marketing was way outside of our comfort zone, but it has been the catalyst for our incredible growth in multiple companies.
- Completely redesigning some of our key websites, in order for them to stay competitive, forced us to rethink our sales and marketing strategies, but allowed us to reposition ourselves and boost our reputation in several industries.

The biggest takeaway that we've learned from pivoting is that we, as business owners, must always be aware of our software's current state and the state of the industry we're in, and we have to be willing to constantly change and adapt in order to stay relevant.

Two times longer

You have to set realistic goals and timelines. If you don't, then you and your team will get disillusioned, lose momentum, and ultimately get burned out. Be honest with the reality of the project, and just know upfront that everything from programming to growth will take two times longer than you plan, and will therefore cost twice as much.

We've mentioned it before, but this has been one of our biggest learning experiences and pain points. In almost every case, what we initially think will be easy, almost always ends up being more complicated, and what we initially think will be quick, almost always end up taking twice as long. This isn't necessarily a bad thing. We just wish we had known it when we started so we could set proper expectations for us and our team.

It's never done

You need to accept the fact that your software will never be completely done. It will continue to improve and evolve year after year. Whether you are on version 1 or version 100, you need to realize that a new version will be on its way. If you understand this, it will help you make better decisions.

One challenge of your software never being done is that you will always have design and development costs. This is why you need to launch as quickly as possible, so you can make enough revenue to cover your fixed costs and expenses.

However, one benefit of your software always improving is that it's much easier for your customers to justify continuing to pay for your service over time. As they see new features and improvements, they are more engaged and will be more likely to stay, so make sure you let them know what changes you're making and how it will benefit them.

One project at a time

When you're first starting out, it's very important that you focus on just one software project at a time. If you're building one software product, and you start building another product, you are going to get into real trouble. As a rule of thumb, you shouldn't start another software project until your first one is making more money than it costs to run, and you have systems in place and a team that you trust that can continue to run it at a profit.

Over the years, we have become very good at automation and putting the right people in key positions in order to allow us to start new projects, but it took us a lot of time, focus and discipline to be able to reach that point. If your first software project isn't profitable before you start the next one, then you are accelerating your losses with no revenues to offset them, which is a bad place to be in.

Avoid business or investment partners

You're probably starting to feel like we're beating a dead horse when it comes to avoiding partners, but we're doing it for your own good. In rare occasions, having an equity partner can be a blessing and a huge advantage, but in most cases, having partners can be your biggest obstacle, and your ultimate downfall. We have both had good and bad partnerships, and we want to protect you, or at least make you aware of the potential issues.

Here are some of the top suggestions we have if you do decide to give someone equity or ownership in your business:

- **Find someone that compliments your skills and abilities.** One of the reasons that we work so well together is that our skill sets are very complementary. Here's a breakout of our individual skills:
  - Garrett (builder): naturally organized and effectively manages projects and teams
  - Scott (visionary): highly creative and comes up with innovative concepts, ideas, and solutions to problems
- **Find someone that is willing to work just as hard as you do.** One of the fastest ways for a partnership to die is for one of the partners to work less than the other. It quickly leads to frustration and resentment. If you bring on a partner you both have to be 100% invested no matter what happens.
- **Create a written agreement with specific expectations for each partner.** Write down exactly what each partner's responsibilities are and what is expected. It also is a good idea to add equity milestones or certain conditions that need to be met, or at least a way to retain your equity if your new partner doesn't pull their weight.
- **Try giving equity upon sale rather than ownership, if possible.** (Refer back to chapter 3 where we talked about this in depth.) If this won't work, then base equity on milestones, but make sure you have the final say on all major decisions.
- **Communicate constantly.** Set up daily or at least weekly meetings to talk with your partners and don't hold anything

back. If things get heated, take a break and come back at a later time to talk things through. Walks are always good to clear your head and solve problems, both alone and with your partners.

Raise your prices

In every one of our businesses we have raised prices multiple times. Back in 2010, when we launched Shopper Approved, we sold it for a fixed monthly price of $12.95/mo. Now we use a pay-as-you-grow model, with our lowest price starting at $199/mo and going up into the thousands per month range depending on the client. Ironically, regardless of the company, almost every time we raise our prices, our sales continue to increase and our churn rates go down.

So don't be scared to raise your prices.

One thing that we have done to help ease the pain for our existing clients, is that we usually grandfather them in at the pricing that they originally signed up under. This makes them happy because they feel like they're getting a deal, it increases their stickiness and lifetime value because they don't want to lose their lower pricing, and it shows them that we're not just in it for the money, which helps to build a long-term relationship that opens the door for us to market future software products to them.

Always be aware of your finances

A huge mistake we made early on is that we had no idea where things were financially. We knew money was coming in and going out (mostly the latter), but that was about it. We based all our decisions on money we thought was there, but usually wasn't, and it cost us dearly.

Nowadays we meet with our bookkeepers for each business each month, and go over all the revenue and all the expenses. We also look at our growth rates, our Monthly Recurring Revenue (MRR), our churn rates, and any other stats we can get our hands on so that we are intimate with the pulse and health of each business. Our goal is to make sure that each company is financially independent and actively growing. Actively managing our finances has helped us make better decisions in hiring staff and growing our software empire.

Do not let this slip by you like it did us. Even if your business is in its infancy, get a bookkeeper ASAP. You will thank us later.

Also, when starting out, always make sure to put 25% of all your net profits (before you pay yourself) in a separate account for taxes. This way, your personal taxes and your business taxes are both covered. If you don't consciously and proactively set aside taxes, then you'll likely spend the money, and you'll be in big trouble when tax season comes around.

Know your billing system

When it comes to recurring billing, it is so important that you have a reliable billing system. We've built systems from scratch and we've paid for existing systems, and are still trying to figure out the best solution.

It doesn't take a rocket scientist to figure out that if your billing system doesn't properly bill your clients, or if your customers don't update their credit cards, then you will lose money.

Here are the essential items you need:

- **A great billing system** - we highly suggest using Stripe.com as your merchant account to handle your recurring billing. Their API is amazing and it's really fast and easy to get approved and create a Stripe account. Plus, both Software Funnels and Click-Funnels are already built to run on Stripe.

- **A great dunning system** - a dunning system is an automated process that alerts your customers if their credit cards fails or expires. Make sure that the billing system you choose has a dunning system in place - it will significantly help with churn and will lower your support costs.

- **A great reporting system** - you need to always be aware of your monthly revenue increases and decreases. ClickFunnels and Software Funnels both have Analytics tools that work with Stripe to help you know all your key indicators and financial numbers.

Bottom line, missed billing cycles, expired credit cards and cancellations all make holes in your bucket, which makes it that much harder to fill it. By knowing the ins and outs of your billing system, you are able to plug the holes and accelerate your growth.

Buying existing software or using open source

Something that we've recently started doing that we wish we would have done in our earlier years is buying existing software or applications. If you can find a product in your market that already exists and you can purchase the software or license the software, this can significantly speed up the development process.

This does cost money but can be totally worth it. For example, with CustomerRewards.com we decided we had to focus our first version on a specific clientele that uses Magento as their shopping cart platform, which meant that we needed to build a Magento extension. However, we didn't have a lot of experience with Magento and we knew it would be our biggest bottleneck. We decided that we could either start from scratch, or find an existing Magento extension and purchase it.

We decided to do some research and we found an amazing extension, so we sent them an email and asked if they would be willing to sell us a copy of their code. After negotiating, it ended up costing us $30,000, but it was exactly what we needed and probably cut our development time by at least six months or more.

Another option is to build your software on existing open source code. This can get a little tricky on the legal end of things so you want to make sure you talk to an open source lawyer to make sure you set things up correctly. This is one of the big secrets behind how we were able to create Software Funnels in record time and have it be so amazing.

Hire a sales team

One mistake we unknowingly made early on is that we didn't hire a sales team. For years we did all our marketing online through Search Engine Optimization (SEO) and Pay-Per-Click (PPC), and our businesses grew very slowly, (keep in mind that ClickFunnels didn't exist back then). However, since we discovered the power of outbound sales, the companies that we've implemented sales teams for have grown exponentially, because we have sales people actively reaching out and engaging directly with business owners, and selling them our software.

It's like Christmas every day!

Another mistake we made, particularly for Cart Rocket, was that we got overly ambitious and tried to build our sales team too fast, before we'd proven our sales processes for that business, and we lost $50,000 in less than three months.

When you're building a sales team for any new software business, we suggest you start with one sales agent and figure out the processes for bringing that particular product to your market. This takes time, but once you have figured it out, and the numbers are solid and show that you can scale, then and only then should you start adding more sales agents. But even then, we suggest you build slowly at first. Try to have each salesperson make enough recurring sales to cover their base wage before hiring the next one. That way, you are always working in the black.

We are always optimizing our sales team and our processes, but here is what we believe to be the ideal set up:

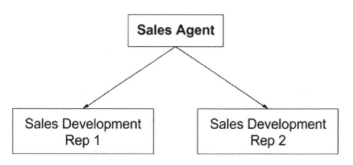

We call this set up a 'sales pod'. Once you get one pod working efficiently, then you go out and hire another pod, and so on. A sales pod is the smallest fully functioning sales team you can have. You can have a pod with only one SDR, but any smaller than that and you only have a sales agent. That means they have no accountability partner, and no one to help them generate warm leads, which makes them very inefficient. The great thing about a pod is that it's very low overhead and the costs are predictable, which allows you to dial in your numbers and break even faster.

The SDRs work throughout the day to set up demos, calls, webinars, etc. for the sales agent they are assigned to. They have access to the sales agent's calendar and are able to set up appointments for them.

If you decide to go down the path of outbound sales, you sales agents will need to be able to demonstrate your product live and in person. This is called a live demo. There are several live demo software services online, but the three that we use are GoToMeeting. com, Zoom.us and Join.me.

When you first start out, your sales agent plays double duty as the sales manager. Part of their responsibilities are to manage the sales team, track the team's progress, and keep innovating and trying new things. Eventually, if they prove worthy, that first sales agent will become the actual sales manager who will oversee the entire sales department.

When it comes to paying your sales team, we've found that starting out with a base wage and commission is best, and then, if possible, moving them to commission only. With Shopper Approved, our top salespeople actually asked us if they could move to commission only. On one hand, they make a lot more money than they used to, but on the other hand, they have no safety net, so they work incredibly hard because they know it's feast or famine. This has had a very positive ripple effect, because since switching to commission only, their sales have increased, which means more recurring revenue for the company. It's a win-win. Now, obviously, the ability to offer commission only is based on your pricing model, but if you ever reach that point, you know you've got a winner.

We can't really tell you what you should pay your SDRs and sales agents, since it largely depends on your target market, your demographics, and your pricing, but we have found that if you want great people, you need to pay top dollar in most cases.

You may think that your product can't be sold via a call center – that's what we thought too. But it wasn't until we took the risk, spent the money, and put resources into a sales team that our businesses really took off.

The reason call centers are so powerful is that you get to talk directly to the people that make the decisions, one on one. Think about it – you are literally seconds away from pitching to anyone in the world with an outbound sales team, and you get their full attention for as long as they're on the phone. That's incredibly powerful!

(We go into a lot more detail about our outbound sales processes in our Software Secrets Training System. To learn more about it, go to www.SoftwareSecrets.com/training)

Only Hire Rock Stars

When we were first starting out, we made a lot of hiring mistakes. But over time, we've come up with a very effective hiring process. What we've found over the years is that there are rock stars and donkeys (we got the phrase 'donkeys' from Dave Ramsey). Our goal at this point is to only hire rock stars and weed out the donkeys. Hiring rock stars takes a bit more work, but it makes all the difference in your company's success.

Rock stars are naturally self-motivated, they are hard workers, and they get stuff done without being micromanaged. They are also way less dramatic, and when there is an issue, they will usually own it and fix it.

Here is our top secret process to hiring great people for any job...

1. Place ad. There are a number of different job sites you can post your job on. We use Indeed.com, Monster.com and local job sites. When posting your ad, it needs to be eye catching and exciting, specify the job details, and state any requirements you may have (e.g. two years experience, bachelors degree, etc.) - all without being too wordy or overwhelming.

2. Create an Application Questionnaire. All of our ads are sent to our application that we post on Breezy.hr which is a software tool that allows us to easily manage applicants and helps us create an application and questionnaire form. For an applicant to even get into our process they must complete the application and questionnaire. Here is an example questionnaire:

Good Afternoon,

In order to help us determine if we're a good fit for each other, please take a few minutes and fill out the questionnaire below.

Question 1 - Are you able to work full-time? (40hrs/week)

Question 2 - Are you able to work at our office in downtown Ogden?

Question 3 - Do you have reliable transportation to get to work?

Question 4 - Are you currently working? If 'Yes' when would you be able to start?

Question 5 - Do you have at least 1 year of _____ experience?

Question 6 - Please explain your online technical skills (ex. Internet, Email, Project Management tools, Google Drive/docs)

Question 7 - We're looking into several candidates for this position. Why should we hire you rather than someone else?

(You can view the digital version at www.SoftwareSecrets.com/questions)

3. Review applications. Once the applicant completes the application, we are able to look at their answers and review their resume. We are VERY picky about resumes, and we only respond to resumes that match our requirements and look like a good fit. We are also big sticklers for presentation and cover letters. Applicants get big points for customizing their cover letters and resumes to match our job requirements.

4. Typing test. To those applicants who look like they'd be a good fit, we send them a follow up email, where we ask them to do a typing test and then take a screenshot and email it to us. Here's an example of the typing test instructions:

Good Afternoon,

We received your application and are interested in moving you to the next step of our hiring process.

Here are the steps you need to take right now to continue with your application for the {position name here} position:

Step 1: Go to this website - http://www.typingtest.com/

Step 2: Select "2-Minute Test" and then select "The Wonderful Wizard of Oz" then click "Start Typing Test"

Step 3: Take a screenshot of your results

Step 4: Email your results to {email here} and make sure to add your full name in the subject line of the email

Once you have followed these steps and you have 40 wpm or higher results we will then send you an email with the next step of our hiring process.

Thank you,
{your representative's name}
{your company's name}

(You can view the digital version at www.SoftwareSecrets.com/email)

This is such a simple step, but there are a lot of donkeys who won't take the time to do it, and they naturally weed themselves out.

5. Voicemail interview. If they complete the typing test and follow the instructions, we send them another email with instructions to call and record a voicemail interview.

We typically send an email similar to this:

Thank you for completing the Typing Test.

The next step is to do a Voicemail Interview. We know this may be something that you have never done before but this allows us to see how you will interact with clients over the phone.

Basically, this means you call the number we give you below and you leave a voicemail.

The key is to follow the steps exactly as we lay them out below.

Here is the number to call and leave a voicemail - {phone number here}

Here are the exact steps to follow:

Step 1 - Tell us your name

Step 2 - Give us your life story in 90 seconds

Step 3 - Pretend like you work for our company as a sales agent, and you just called a potential client and got to a gatekeeper. You are trying to get to the Sr. VP of Marketing. For fun, go ahead and role play what you would do, (just pretend that the client is answering back any questions you ask, and be creative).

All of this needs to be done in less than 5 minutes.

Thank you,
{your representative's name}
{your company's name}

---

*(You can view the digital version at
www.SoftwareSecrets.com/voicemail)*

The example above was for a sales agent position, but you can do it for any position, you just have to change step 3 to a role play scenario that fits that particular job.

The reason for this part of the hiring process is again to weed out the donkeys that won't do something a little bit outside of their comfort zone. This is different than what normal companies do, but we believe that it is essential to hiring the best people possible. Again, if they aren't willing to get on the phone for a few minutes and answer a couple of questions, how can you expect them to do difficult or uncomfortable things related to their job?

The easiest way to set up this step is to create a Skype number or a Google Voice account with a voicemail option, and then on your message, just tell them to follow the steps that were emailed to them, and they simply record their interview after the beep.

6. Phone interview. If the applicant completes the voicemail interview, and we like their answers and think they will be a good fit, we move them to the phone interview step. If you already have a manager, they can do this interview, along with everything else up to this point. During the phone interview, specific questions should be asked about their work history, their resume, their voicemail interview, or anything else necessary to qualify them for the position.

7. Face-to-face interview. If the phone interview goes well, then it's time to have the applicant come in for a face-to-face interview (or over Zoom.us or Skype if they are remote). If you have a manager, they should do this interview on their own. If you don't have one, go to the next step.

8. Face-to-face interview with the owners. If a candidate makes it this far, they have a very good chance of being hired. At the end of this interview, if you plan on hiring them, then invite them and their spouse for lunch or dinner, (if they don't have a spouse or significant other, then just have lunch or dinner with the candidate).

9. Lunch or dinner interview. When you hire someone, you are making a major commitment to each other, so you need to be somewhat aware of the candidate's private life. If their significant other appears to be high maintenance, or you get a bad vibe when meeting them, then it might not be a good fit. It's better to find out now and cut ties than to suffer later. This interview is also a good opportunity to see how someone acts in a more personal, intimate environment.

10. Decision time. Don't rush this. If you decide to hire someone, make sure that they know what expectations they need to meet. Once you do decide to pull the trigger, create an employment agreement that states your expectations in plain, easy to understand terms. This agreement needs to be signed by you and the new employee.

So there you have it! You are welcome to change any of the steps to match your particular needs, but this is our hiring process and it's been highly effective.

Before we implemented this process, we would pretty much hire anyone that looked decent and had a pulse. But over time, we realized that we didn't just want good people – we wanted rock stars! We didn't want to settle for anything less than amazing, top-quality winners who were willing to roll up their sleeves and work hard to make our companies successful.

Since we made that decision, our company has changed significantly for the better. We are literally surrounded by incredible, fun, happy, energetic, boy band loving (that's for you, Eric), out-of-the-box thinking, problem solving, self-motivated rock stars all day long, and it's amazing!

(Note: You can still hire people that are personally recommended by friends or colleagues using this method - just be sure to hold them to the same standards as everyone else, and if they don't complete the process, then you know they're a donkey.)

Now, you're probably thinking, "That's so much work to hire some-one." Well, you're right, but besides only wanting to work with rock stars, there are two other very compelling reasons why we have such a rigorous hiring process:

1. It actually saves us time and is less work than the traditional hiring process, because we don't have to interview 20 'good' people. Most of the initial steps are really quick and easy to manage, and they instantly weed out all the donkeys.

   Surprisingly, we've found that anyone less than a rock star won't even complete the very simple, initial steps in the process. And if they aren't willing to go through and complete the initial steps, then it stands to reason that they probably aren't willing to follow through on things you'll need them to do as an employee.

2. Turnover is a huge pain and costs a lot of money. We want people that are going to contribute and stay with our company long-term. We've found that rock stars stay longer because they have a natural instinct to play to win. They want to see the company succeed, and they take pride in being a part of that success.

Work 'on' your business, not 'in' your business

At first, you're going to wear a lot of hats in your business. You'll be the CEO, CFO, CMO, CTO, Customer Service Manager and much more. However, the sooner you can start working 'on' your business instead of 'in' it, the better.

Working 'on' your business allows you to see the 10,000 foot view, instead of seeing your business from the ground view 'in' the trenches. When you're working 'on' your business, the perspective and view are very different. It's this larger view and perspective that allow you to improve, pivot and grow exponentially.

The way we do this is that we hire a true bonafide rock star as the Operations Manager to run the day-to-day operations of each business we build. Someone that we can trust to fight in the trenches, take on big challenges, and work effectively 'in' the business.

This allows us to go on our daily walks, have high-level meetings, improve our processes, make important decisions, and most importantly focus 'on' each of our businesses.

The reality is, that until you make the transition from working 'in' your business, to 'on' your business, you will be the bottleneck in your business, and your growth and success will be limited.

One way that we work 'on' our business is our Monday Mastermind meetings. This is where we don't even sit at our desks when we get into the office. Instead, we go straight into our conference room and talk about all of our businesses from a 10,000 foot view. As part of our mastermind, we go over what we call our 6 P's, which are; Product, Process, Promotion, People, Profits, and Philanthropy.

In our Software Secrets Training System, we go into a lot more detail about working 'on' your business, and we break down the 6 P's, which really helps us to organize our priorities and action items for the week. To learn more, go to www.SoftwareSecrets.com/training.

Have fun and give back

It took us a few years, but after a certain point in our careers, we began to ask ourselves, "Why did we get into the software business in the first place?" After several walks and high-level discussions about life, we ultimately decided that the answer to why we build software was so that we could have freedom, money, give back to the world, and have fun.

At this point we have plenty of freedom and money. What really motivates us nowadays is giving back, and we've had some incredible experiences giving back by building schools in Kenya, helping orphanages in Kenya and Guatemala, and supporting various feeding programs around the world. But that's just the tip of the iceberg. Our future plans include many more philanthropic projects and adventures. To us, giving back is the ultimate reward, and building software is simply a means to an end, but we are absolutely loving the journey!

The last reason why we got into the software business was so we could have fun, and we have a lot of it. We have multiple offices in Ogden, Utah, and we take our teams out to lunch on a regular basis. We go to movies. We go go-karting. We go to concerts. And in our offices we have things like dart boards, Love Sacs, hoverboards, basketball, pool, ping pong, and putting greens. We also have fully stocked kitchens with all kinds of goodies – and of course, green smoothies.

Epilogue
by Scott Brandley

was born and raised in Alberta, Canada. And ever since I was a child, I wanted to be like my dad. Over the years, he taught me 3 very important principles that I've tried to live my life by, which are: Think big. Work hard. Never give up.

Think big

Some of my earliest memories involve watching my dad come up with big ideas, and then trying to make them a reality. Things like:

- Building a giant waterpark, with the main attraction being a huge cement dome with waterslides weaving in and out of it. My dad was a draftsman by trade, and domes used to be cool. I remember him drawing incredible pictures of the 'Water Dome' that made my imagination run wild. He and his brothers spent years trying to make this idea happen, but ultimately it didn't pan out.

- Partnering with Shasta beverages to transport pure glacier water from British Columbia to the US in big tanker trucks, and then bottling it - decades before bottled water ever took off. This idea had huge potential, but to pull it off he needed partners. Unfortunately, the partners he brought on didn't fulfill their part of the agreement and the deal fell through.

■ Designing and building a super energy-efficient home. My dad had never built a house before, but he came up with a radical new design based on cutting edge technologies at the time, and so he designed it, drew up the plans, figured out how to become his own contractor, and then built it from scratch with his brothers. If you ask me, it was the coolest house in the whole town.

■ Creating a discount coupon book that could be sold as a fundraiser for the Scouting program. This idea actually took off back when I was around 9 years old. My dad called the coupon company 'Spree'. This was in the mid 80's, and it had never been done before in Southern Alberta. My dad spent weeks going from store to store and selling business owners on the concept. Then he designed the book, got it printed, and got the Scouts on board to sell it. I still remember my dad pouring thousands of coupon books into a huge pile on the living room floor, next to another huge pile of vinyl book covers that we had to put on each book by hand.

The crazy thing is that these were just the ideas he had before I was 10 years old. He came up with several other ideas while I was a teenager. Some were successful and some weren't, but that didn't stop him from thinking big, and it has inspired me to do the same.

Work hard

As long as I can remember, my dad taught me the importance of hard work, but there was one particular experience that I distinctly remember as a child that taught me this life lesson.

When I was 8, I registered for my first Cub Scout Pinewood Derby. I designed a race car. My dad helped me cut it out, and then he gave me some wood files and sandpaper and told me to start sanding it. I remember sanding that car for what seemed like days on end. Each time I thought I was done, I would go ask him, "Dad, is this good enough?" He would kindly tell me that I needed to keep sanding, and send me back outside. Once I had finally sanded the car to perfection, we painted it a high gloss cherry red, and he helped me put some pinstriping on it. It looked amazing!

When we pulled up to the Pinewood Derby, the parking lot was full. It was huge event with well over a hundred boys in attendance from all over Southern Alberta. The track was so big that the adults had climb up on a platform to set up the cars.

I still remember anxiously waiting in anticipation as they put my car up on the track next to the other competitors. They pulled the lever, and the cars raced toward the finish line. My little red race car blew every other car away as if they were standing still! It was thrilling to watch!

As the morning went on, my car continued to win heat after heat, until there were only 6 cars left. I thought my heart was going to pound out of my chest! They lined up the cars for the final heat, pulled the lever, and I watched my little car race down the track and win! It was one of the most exciting days of my childhood, and to this day I attribute it to my dad making me sand that car for hours and hours. As a little boy it seemed like a herculean effort, but the hard work paid off in the end - and it's something that I've tried to apply throughout my life.

Never give up

This is probably the most important lesson my dad taught me.

Over the course of my life, my dad has had a lot of different business ideas. With each idea, it's almost as if he's in a baseball game, and he picks up his bat and goes out to the batter's box. Many times he's struck out. Occasionally he's hit ground balls and made it to first or second base. But, there have been a few times in his life, where he's gone up to bat and has hit a home run!

But, as exciting as the home runs were, the lesson was taught in those hard times when he was out. No matter what happened, he would dust himself off, pick up his bat, and head back to take another swing. The reality is that the home runs can never happen in life, if you don't keep going up to bat and swinging.

My dad was my first mentor

Throughout my life, I have always looked up to my dad as a mentor. To me a mentor is someone that teaches you important life lessons, and motivates and inspires you to do better or be better, and he did that for me.

When I was 21 years old, my dad and I became business partners and started our first online business together selling clothing & apparel, (which we mentioned at the beginning of the book). This was back in 1997, when the internet was brand new. Even though we had no idea what we were doing, we applied the three principles of thinking big, working hard, and never giving up to our new online store, and within a few years, our website took off, and we started selling hundreds of thousands of dollars a year in online retail sales.

And the rest, as they say, is history...

In 2004, my dad and I sold our online apparel company and decided to go into software.

In 2006, my dad and I launched our first major SAAS company, TrustGuard.com, which opened our eyes to the incredible potential and power of recurring billing.

In 2008, I met Garrett.

In 2009, Garrett and I started working together, building Shopper Approved as a skunkworks project for the software company that my dad and I started in 2004. We also did some side projects together.

In 2010, after launching Shopper Approved, Garrett and I officially became business partners, and have continued to build and launch incredible software products ever since.

Looking back, I am very grateful to my dad for taking me under his wing and mentoring me. I truly believe that if he wouldn't have taught me the three principles of thinking big, working hard, and never giving up, I don't know if I would be where I am today.

The importance of mentors

Over the years, Garrett and I have continued to seek out mentors, and we've been incredibly blessed and privileged to learn from some of the best, including: Andy Jenkins, Alex Mandossian, David Frey, Armand Morin, Stu McLaren, T. Harv Eker, Tony Robbins, and of course, Russell Brunson.

We have learned so much from each of these industry and thought leaders, not only from reading their books and taking their courses, but from becoming their friends and spending quality time with many of them. We've been on adventures with them, gone to seminars and mastermind events with them, had dinner with them, brainstormed new ideas with them, visited with several of them in their homes, and have even spent time with some of their families.

With the help of these special mentors, the experiences we've had, and lessons they've taught us, we've been able to become better leaders, builders, innovators, team players, planners, problem solvers, and most importantly, better entrepreneurs.

Ultimately, we wrote the book Software Secrets, because we want to be your mentors.

We want to give to you what each of our mentors have given to us, which is the precious gift of knowledge and experience.

Hopefully, by reading this book, we've helped to open your eyes to the incredible, limitless possibilities and opportunities that software provides.

We hope that we've changed the way that you think about making money, and how by combining software with the exponential power of recurring billing, you can generate tens of thousands, hundreds of thousands, or even millions of dollars each month, month after month, year after year, for the rest of your life.

But most importantly, we hope that we've ignited a massive fire under you, and that you can't stop thinking about starting your own software business!

Now that you've read the entire Software Secrets book, you have reached a unique crossroads of sorts. At this point, you ultimately have 3 paths that you can take from here on your software journey:

1. **You can start with what you've learned so far.** If all you do is take the information you've learned in this book, and follow the principles we've taught you, you'll avoid many of the software mistakes and pitfalls that most people make, and you'll significantly shorten your learning curve. This is the best education you can possibly get for under $20 bucks.

2. **You can continue your software education.** If you're serious about starting a software business and you want to take things to the next level, you can watch us as we build our lat-

est breakthrough software company, Software Funnels, from conception to launch. Our Software Secrets Training System is jam-packed with training videos, podcasts, checklists, blog posts, special breakout sessions, a private Facebook group that we are actively involved in, and everything else you need to accelerate your software development and maximize your opportunity for success. Simply follow our lead as we walk you through the steps and show you what to do. Go to www.SoftwareSecrets.com/training to see if it's right for you.

3. **You can hire us to help you get started.** This option definitely isn't for everyone, but if money's not an issue, and you want Garrett and I to be your personal mentors, we offer both 1 and 2-day individual mastermind sessions, where we meet with you at our main office in Ogden, Utah, and help you to brainstorm, mind map, and wireframe your entire software project. We even line up your design team and your programming team, set up your servers, optimize your Software Funnels account, and personally train you on how to effectively manage your project. We typically charge $15,000 for one day or $25,000 for two days. If this sounds like something you'd be interested in, go to www.SoftwareSecrets.com/mentor and fill out the short application form.

In closing, Garrett and I want to personally thank you for reading our book. Software Secrets has been a labor of love for both of us, and we've literally put hundreds of hours into writing it. It's the culmination of our professional life's work to date, and we sincerely hope that it changes your life for the better.

If this book does make a difference in your life, please let us know. The best gift you could ever give us is to send us an email about your personal software journey. We'd love to hear from you. And if you send us your story, we not only promise to write back, but we'll also share your experience with our team, and we'll post it on our Software Secrets blog so you can be an inspiration to others. Please send your email to mysoftwarestory@softwaresecrets.com.

Where will software take you? It's time to find out.

Sincerely,

Scott Brandley